RUNNING THE NUMBERS

A STEP-BY-STEP GUIDE TO LIFE'S MAJOR
FINANCIAL DECISIONS

MICHAEL A. TORTORICH

MICHAEL TORTORICH FINANCE

Visit the website at MichaelTortorichFinance.com

ISBN: 978-1-7367575-0-5 (paperback)

ISBN: 978-1-7367575-1-2 (e-book)

Published by Desert Press Books

CONTENTS

PREFACE

As a father of two young children, I often struggle with how to teach my kids financial literacy. To help them associate earning money with hard work, like most parents I give them chores or reward them for good grades in school. You can often hear me saying, "Money doesn't grow on trees!" While those are all good ways to instill best practices, true financial literacy comes from understanding how to run the numbers. After thinking long and hard about how to educate my kids, I knew the best way was to consolidate all the financial lessons I had learned in one place and present those lessons to them in an organized and thoughtful way. So, I decided to write a book.

My goal was to have something to give them, a playbook so to speak, from which they could learn important financial concepts and, more importantly, how to think through key financial decisions. But as I progressed in writing the book, it became something much bigger. I realized that the concepts and lessons I was trying to teach were crucial not just to my kids, but to everyone, and I became determined to spread the word.

All my life I've had a burning curiosity around finance, which is the study of money and investments. At its most basic level, money is what we use to buy things, but it goes so much deeper than that. Over the course of completing my undergraduate degree and MBA, I learned how important having a basic understanding of finance is to every single one of us. Understanding compound interest for a credit card, financing for the purchase of a car or house, basic budgeting, or investment analysis can make the difference between constantly being in debt and financial freedom.

Many of the concepts and calculations I outline in the book I learned through getting my MBA, and some just through life experience. But you shouldn't have to get an MBA to prepare yourself for important financial decisions. I believe one of the major problems with our school system is a lack of financial education. We expect our high school graduates to be well rounded, and why that doesn't include a proper financial education is beyond me. Not to say that other subjects aren't important: experts in all fields make great contributions to society. The truth, however, is that a number of subjects are not applicable to most people outside of an academic setting. On the other hand, a financial education is crucial in preparing yourself to be an adult in the real world.

Using my own experiences, I organized this book in order of how most people will encounter important financial milestones. The idea is not for you to read the book one time and become a financial expert. Depending on where you are in life the first time you read the book, many of the scenarios I outline may not even apply to you. But eventually you are likely to come across all of the situations I describe. The intention is for you to use this book as a guide that you can continually refer to, throughout your life, as you encounter these important financial decisions.

Additional Items of Note

1. Website Resources: To enhance the learning experience, I recommend familiarizing yourself with the additional resources on my website (MichaelTortorichFinance.com). These additional resources are as follows:
    *   YouTube Series: Each video corresponds to a chapter or section in the book. The videos allow me to give additional color around the topics and examples covered where it was not practical to do so in the book. Links to all available videos can be found on my website in the "Media" section or by searching "MichaelTortorichFinance" on YouTube.
    *   Backup Excel: Each example in the book has a corresponding tab with the detailed calculations in an Excel workbook that can be found on my website in the "Excel" section. The password to download the file can be found in the "Final Thoughts" section at the end of this book.

2. Glossary: As there may be many unfamiliar terms throughout the book, I have added a glossary in the back for reference. All words in italics can be found in the glossary.

3. Reading Order: I recommend reading the chapters in order as the later chapters build on concepts introduced in chapters one through five. Additionally, I cannot emphasize enough the importance of the first two chapters ("Time Value of Money" and "Compound Interest"). Making sure you have a firm understanding of these concepts is key to following the rest of the examples in the book.

4. Rounding: Please note, where possible all numbers are rounded to the nearest dollar.

5. Data Tables: All shaded cells denote inputs. In the accompanying Excel these input cells can be changed and the formulas will automatically refresh.

6. General Comments: Finance is an extremely broad subject with an infinite number of rabbit holes, and there is no way I can explore, in complete detail, every topic. As such, to keep the content I cover manageable, the scope of each topic is not all encompassing. Reading this book will give you a very good understanding of personal finance, but there will always be additional levels of detail you can explore. I have purposefully added many references to other websites and organizations and have included a "Recommended Reading & Additional Resources" section in the book. Financial literacy is a journey, and I encourage you to explore further any topic that interests you.

ACKNOWLEDGMENTS

To my loving wife:
Thank you from the bottom of my heart for all the support that goes into keeping the machine that is our household running. Without you none of this would have been possible.

To my beautiful children:
I want to apologize for all the times I said "in a minute" when you asked me to play with you. As an adult you are always busy with something, but that is never an excuse. Time is something you make, and while it is often difficult to make time for everything I would like, I want you to know that I am always thinking of you.

To Luke Ishihara, Elaine Lim, and Jose Valbuena:
Thank you for reviewing my first draft. Your suggestions and critiques added significant value and without a doubt improved the quality of this book.

1

TIME VALUE OF MONEY

A re you familiar with the saying "A bird in the hand is worth two in the bush"? Well, that's the basic concept behind 'time value' of money. A dollar today is worth more than a dollar tomorrow. This is due to two reasons: *inflation* and *risk*.

Perhaps you heard your grandparents say, "Back in my day a movie ticket used to cost fifty cents, and now it's fifteen bucks to go to a movie!" That's inflation. It's the fact that prices rise over time and that a dollar in the future is worth less than a dollar today because you can purchase less with it. Risk is uncertainty of outcome. In this case, the 'uncertainty of outcome' is the risk of not being paid back for any money that you lend.

Let's work through an example to put these two concepts together. Say you agree to loan $10,000 and it will be paid back one year from today. Would you lend the money if you were only going to be paid back the original $10,000? Well, you shouldn't! This is because prices will have increased a year from now and you will need to be paid back the amount you lent plus some additional amount so that your purchasing power stays the same.

Let's say you expect inflation to be 4% (i.e., what you can purchase today for $10,000 will cost you an additional $400 [$10,000 * 4%] a year from now). In this case, you would require $10,400 in one year. But what about the risk of you not being paid back? You need to be compensated for that as well. In finance, we call this a *risk premium*. There are many ways to assess a risk premium, and I'll cover some of these in more detail later in the book. For now, let's assume the borrower is trustworthy and use a risk premium of 3%. This means you have to be paid an extra $300 ($10,000 * 3%) in addition to the $10,400 one year from now.

In summary, for the $10,000 you lend today, you will be paid back:

Original Amount	$10,000
Inflation	$400 ┐
	├ Interest
Risk premium	$300 ┘
Total Due in One Year	**$10,700**

The additional $700 that must be paid back is called *interest*, and the *interest rate* is 7% or ($700/$10,000). So, from now on, when you hear the term interest, you know that it is actually made up of two components: inflation and risk. For detailed calculations, see the "*Simple interest*" tab in the accompanying Excel.

2

COMPOUND INTEREST

L et's take the previous example a step further and see what would happen if instead of being paid back one year from now, you will be paid back in two years.

Before we can continue, we need to clarify a couple basic terms:

1. *Period*: This is the frequency at which *interest* is charged. In the previous example, we used one year, but any frequency can be used for the period (e.g., one day, week, month, year …).
2. *Interest rate*: This is what is charged for lending money and is stated as a percentage of the amount owed. In the previous example, we determined the interest rate to be 7% (4% for *inflation* and 3% for *risk premium*).

So, two years from now, how much should you be paid back? The original $10,000 loaned plus $700 for year one and $700 for year two (known as *simple interest*)? No. This is because in the real world, interest is compounded. In other words, interest is charged on interest. So let's work through an actual example.

As we saw from the previous example, the amount owed at the end of one year (period one) is $10,700. To calculate the amount owed at the end of two years (period two), we add another 7% to the *principal* (the $10,000 originally loaned) and interest ($700) at the end of year one ($10,700 * 7% = $749). The total due at the end of two years (period two) is $11,449, not $11,400. The additional $49 is the compounding effect from the interest. For this example, the impact is extremely small because we are only using two periods. If you compound over more periods, the impact is much more pronounced.

Let's look at another example and compare a simple interest calculation with a *compound interest* calculation, but now assume you're going to be paid back in 20 years.

Simple Interest

This charges interest only on the principal amount. The formula and inputs are as follows:

Formula:

Interest

Principal + (Principal * Interest Rate * Number of Periods)

Inputs:

Principal: $10,000
Interest rate: 7%
Periods: 20

Calculation:

$10,000 + ($10,000 * 0.07 * 20) = $10,000 + $14,000 = $24,000

The total amount owed at the end of 20 years is $24,000 ($10,000 principal and $14,000 interest).

Compound Interest

This charges interest on the interest and is how the calculation works in the real world. The formula and inputs are as follows:

Formula:

Principal * $(1 + \text{Interest rate})^{\text{Number of Periods}}$

Inputs:

Principal: $10,000
Interest rate: 7%
Periods: 20

Calculation:

$10,000 * $(1 + 0.07)^{20}$ = $10,000 * 3.87 = $38,679

The total amount owed at the end of 20 years is $38,679 ($10,000 principal and $28,679 interest).

Compared with the previous example of simple interest, compounding slightly more than doubled the amount of interest owed ($28,679 vs. $14,000). For detailed calculations, see the "Simple vs. Compound interest" tab in the accompanying Excel.

If all this seems a bit overwhelming, don't worry. You will have many more opportunities to practice these concepts as we go through additional examples in the book. At this point, the key is to know how compound interest is calculated. And again, I can't emphasize enough the importance of compound interest as it is used in virtually every financial transaction.

3

CREDIT CARDS

Turning 18 comes with a lot of privileges. You are now legally an adult, you can vote, and you can get a credit card in your name. Whether via mail, online, or on a college campus with a free T-shirt, typically as soon as you turn 18, you get bombarded with advertisements to apply for a credit card.

First, let me say that I am not against credit cards. They are very useful; in fact, I can't imagine life without one. However, it's important to know exactly what you are agreeing to when you sign up and what the financial implications of borrowing with one are.

In this chapter, we will do the following:

1. Examine what a credit card is and the implications of using one
2. Discuss pros and cons of credit cards
3. Demystify the fine print
4. Work through examples of how to calculate *interest*
5. Calculate the *minimum payment*
6. Discuss variable *interest rates*
7. Review the basics of a *credit score*

What Is a Credit Card?

Technically, a credit card is just a rectangular piece of plastic that allows you to make purchases without using cash. The more important thing to understand is what actually happens when you use it. When you make a purchase with a credit card, you are actually taking a short-term loan from a bank (whichever bank issued that card). Most people don't think of using their credit card at Starbucks as taking a short-term loan, but that is in fact exactly what you are doing.

Pros and Cons

Without credit cards, we would all be stuck back in the 1960s. There would be no online shopping; we'd still be writing checks and carrying around wads of cash. Credit cards enable us to remote pay for things instantly and, in general, make our day-to-day lives much more convenient. Also, don't forget about the points. Almost all credit cards come with some kind of program that lets you accumulate points to use for plane tickets, hotel stays, restaurants, you name it. I recommend thepointsguy.com as a place to start if you are looking for good reviews to figure out which credit card is right for you.

But credit cards also come with one key drawback: they are an extremely expensive way to borrow money (typically you will pay 15% to 25% interest). If you are disciplined and pay off your balance in full by the statement date, usually you will not be charged interest. However, if you aren't this disciplined, then you better be prepared to pay through the nose in interest and fees. The banks have to get the money for all those awesome point programs from somewhere, right?

Personally I have never charged anything I did not already have the money to pay for. I'm not saying you have to do the same, but I think that's the most responsible and financially prudent thing to do.

Fine Print and Examples

All credit card contracts have two sections that you need to read: "Offer Details" and "Pricing and Terms." The "Offer Details" section will explain how you earn points, what bonus you receive for new signup, and any other perks of the card. This section is pretty self-explanatory and will obviously differ depending on the type of card and the bank you choose.

The "Pricing and Terms" section will detail your interest rate, penalty fees, and how the interest will be charged. There are a lot of scary-sounding terms and percentage rates in this section, so let's break down the key terms you need to know and see how to use them to get a better understanding of what you are really signing up for.

We will review key terms in the following order:

1. *Annual Percentage Rate (APR)*
2. *Annual Percentage Yield (APY)*
3. *Average daily balance vs. daily balance method*
4. Minimum payment

Annual Percentage Rate (APR) and Annual Percentage Yield (APY)

Usually, the first thing you will see is the Annual Percentage Rate (APR). This is the interest rate you will be charged. Most credit cards have a range and will charge you somewhere in that range depending on your credit score (a number based on your financial history that indicates your creditworthiness). Your credit score will also impact the amount you are able to borrow (i.e., your credit limit). In addition, the APR section will specify whether the rate is variable or not. We'll come back to variability and credit score at the end of the chapter, but for now we'll focus on the APR.

APR is the approximate yearly rate you are charged for borrowing money. Let's go through an example to see how this works.

Assumptions:

- APR is 15% and is compounded monthly (i.e., 12 times per year)
- Loan balance is $5,000
- Loan + interest is due after one year

First, let's calculate what the balance due would be using *simple interest* and let's assume on day 1 you charged $5,000 and held that balance for the entire year.

The formula and inputs are as follows:

Formula:
    Principal + (Principal * Interest rate * Number of Periods)

Inputs:
    Principal: $5,000
    Interest rate: 15%
    Periods: 1

Calculation:
    $5,000 + ($5,000 * 0.15 * 1) = $5,000 + $750 = $5,750

The balance due after one year is $5,750 ($5,000 principal and $750 interest).

Now let's calculate what the balance due would be if compounded monthly, again assuming on day 1 you charged $5,000 and held that balance for the entire year.

The APR is stated in annual terms, so the first thing you need to do is figure out what the monthly rate is. To do this you simply divide the APR by 12. So, the monthly rate is 15%/12 = 1.25%. Next, you apply the monthly rate to the principal and any previously accrued interest at the end of each month to get your new balance.

The amount of interest owed at the end of the year, with monthly compounding, is $804, or $54 more than when we used simple interest. The additional $54 ($804 vs. $750) is the result of compounding interest and because of the extra $54, your Annual Percentage Yield (i.e., your effective interest rate) is actually $804/$5,000 = 16.08%, or 1.08% higher than the advertised 15%.

Exhibit 3.1 Annual Percentage Yield (APY) Monthly Compounding Detailed Calculations

APY Calculation

Assumptions	
Principal	$5,000
Annual Percentage Rate	15.00%
Compounding	Monthly
Periodic Rate (15%/12)	1.25%

Compound Interest

	Month 1	Month 2	Month 3		Month 10	Month 11	Month 12
Principal	$5,000	$5,063	$5,126		$5,591	$5,661	$5,732
Interest Formula	$5,000 * 1.25%	$5,063 * 1.25%	$5,126 * 1.25%	......	$5,591 * 1.25%	$5,661 * 1.25%	$5,732 * 1.25%
Interest	$62.50	$63.28	$64.07		$69.89	$70.77	$71.65
Balance at End of Each Month	**$5,063**	**$5,126**	**$5,190**		**$5,661**	**$5,732**	**$5,804**

I made the illustration above so you can see the details behind the compounding, but going forward we will use the formula referenced earlier, in Chapter 2 ("*Compound Interest*"). For this example, the calculations are as follows:

Formula:
  Principal * (1 + Interest rate)$^{\text{Number of Periods}}$

Inputs:
  Principal: $5,000
  Interest rate: 1.25%
  Periods: 12

Calculation:
  $5,000 * (1 + 0.0125)^{12} = \$5,000 * 1.1608 = \$5,804$

The balance due after one year is $5,804 ($5,000 principal and $804 interest).

In summary, if interest is charged more frequently than once per year, your effective interest rate is actually higher than the APR. This is because the interest is being compounded (i.e., interest is being charged on the interest). Understanding this nuance is important as different loans will use different periods for compounding.

Average Daily Balance vs. Daily Balance Method

Let's continue with the previous example and look at the different ways the bank can calculate your interest. In this instance we will look at interest calculated for a one-month billing cycle.

First we need to find the *daily periodic rate (DPR)*. To do this you divide the APR by the number of days in a standard year (if it's a leap year use 366). Some banks use 360 instead of the actual number of days in a year, and this should be specified in the "Pricing and Terms" section of your card agreement. The calculation is as follows:

Inputs:
    Interest rate: 15%
    Periods: 365

Calculation:
    15%/365 = 0.0411%, or 0.000411 in decimal form

This means you will be charged 0.0411% each day on the amount outstanding.

The interest can be calculated in two ways. The bank can apply the daily periodic rate to the average outstanding balance for the month, known as the average daily balance method, or compound interest daily on the outstanding balance, known as the daily balance method.

First, we'll look at an example of how interest is calculated using the average daily balance method.

Let's make a more realistic assumption this time and instead of assuming you charged $5,000 on day 1, we'll assume you started with a zero balance and built up to $5,000 over the month (30 days) as follows:

    Day 1: Spend $1,000
    Day 11: Spend $5,000
    Day 21: Pay $1,000

Your daily balance for days 1–10 is $1,000; for days 11–20, it is $6,000, and for days 21–30, $5,000. Next, to find your average daily balance you take a weighted average of your balances as follows:

    Step 1: ($1,000 * 10) + ($6,000 * 10) + ($5,000 * 10) = $10,000 + $60,000 + $50,000 = $120,000
    Step 2: Divide $120,000 by 30 (the number of days in your billing cycle)

This gives you an average daily balance of $4,000.

Next, to find your interest owed, apply the daily periodic rate to your average daily balance as follows:

Formula:

    Daily Periodic Rate * Average Daily Balance * Number of Days in the Billing Cycle = Interest Charge

Inputs:

    Daily Periodic Rate: 0.0411%, or 0.000411 in decimal form (= 15%/365)
    Average Daily Balance: $4,000
    Periods: 30

Calculation:

    0.000411 * $4,000 * 30 = $49.32

Your interest owed at the end of the month is $49.32, which is less than the $63 of interest calculated at the end of month one in the previous example. This is because you did not have a $5,000 balance outstanding for the entire month (for the first 10 days the outstanding balance was only $1,000). However, as I mentioned in the opening of this chapter, if you pay the balance in full before the statement date you will likely not be charged interest.

Now let's look at the daily balance method.

Let's use the same example as before but now compound the interest daily. We again assume you start the month with a zero balance and build up to $5,000 over the 30-day month as follows:

    Day 1: Spend $1,000
    Day 11: Spend $5,000
    Day 21: Pay $1,000

Because interest is compounding daily we will have to apply the compound interest formula each time the credit card is charged or a payment is made. There will be three stages: days 1–10, 11–20, and 21–30. And because interest is compounding daily, the *period* is the number of days in each stage.

Formula:

    $\text{Principal} * (1 + \text{Interest rate})^{\text{Number of Periods}}$

Days 1–10

Inputs:

    Principal: $1,000
    Interest rate: 0.0411%
    Periods: 10

Calculation:

    $\$1,000 * (1 + 0.000411)^{10} = \$1,000 * 1.00411 = \$1,004.11$

Days 11–20

Inputs:

    Beginning Balance: $1,004.11

    Amount Charged (Paid): $5,000.00

    Interest rate: 0.0411%

    Periods: 10

Calculation:

    $6004.11 * (1 + 0.000411)^{10} = \$6004.11 * 1.00411 = \$6,028.83$

Days 21–30

Inputs:

    Beginning Balance: $6,028.83

    Amount Charged (Paid):   ($1,000.00)

    Interest rate: 0.0411%

    Periods: 10

Calculation:

    $5,028.83 * (1 + 0.000411)^{10} = \$5,028.83 * 1.00411 = \$5,049.54$

Your interest owed at the end of the month is $49.54. Compared with using the average daily balance method, using the daily balance method (where interest compounds daily) results in additional interest of $0.22 ($49.54 vs. $49.32).

The math for the daily balance method is a bit tedious, and the objective here is not for you to be an expert in these calculations. The key takeaway is that this method is more expensive. For detailed calculations see the "Credit Card Payment" tab in the accompanying Excel.

Even though the impact at an individual level isn't much (in this example it's only $0.22 per month), the reason there are two ways of calculating the interest is because for a large institution (such as a large bank) this seemingly small tweak in the formula can have a big impact on the bottom line. For example, if a bank has 20 million credit card customers, each paying an extra 22 cents per month in interest, it adds up to $52,800,000 ($0.22 * 20,000,000 * 12) in profits at the end of the year.

Minimum Payment

You've probably heard people say, "Don't just make your credit card's minimum payment or you will never pay it off." While this is not always the case, 99% of the time if you make only the minimum payment you will indeed never pay your credit card off. This is because the interest is usually more than your minimum payment. Minimum payments vary by card and are typically the larger of 1% of your balance or a minimum dollar amount (usually $25 to $50). Let's continue with the previous example, using the average daily balance method, where interest is calculated on your average outstanding balance for the month, and see what actually happens if you make only the minimum payment.

For this example we will assume the minimum payment is the larger of $35 or 1% of your average daily balance. Also, we know, from our previous calculation, the average daily balance for the month is $4,000 and the daily periodic rate (assuming an APR of 15% and using 365 days in the year) is 0.0411%.

To calculate the minimum payment you compare $35 with 1% of $4,000, which is $40 ($4,000 * 1%). Since $40 is the larger of the two amounts, the minimum payment is $40. Per the previous calculations, the interest for the month is $49.32, which is more than your required minimum payment. So if you pay only the minimum, you will have paid none of the principal down. And if you continue to pay only the minimum, not only will you never pay down the principal, but the amount owed will increase every month.

Variable Interest Rates

To make things even more complicated banks often use a variable interest rate (i.e., a variable APR). I will not do any calculations in this section, but I do want to explain how a variable rate is built up and where the components come from.

In the "Pricing and Terms" of a credit card agreement, the APR section usually reads something like this: "APR is X% to Y% based on your creditworthiness. APR will vary with the market based on the *prime rate* (also sometimes referred to as a base rate)." In other words, an APR is built up of two components: the prime rate and a *risk premium*.

The prime rate is a benchmark rate that banks use to lend to their most creditworthy customers (usually big companies and not individuals). This rate varies month to month with the market, and most major countries have their own prime rate. For example, the US prime rate can be found in the "Money Rates" section of the *Wall Street Journal*, and the base rate, in the UK, can be found on the Bank of England's website.

The risk premium depends on your specific creditworthiness and is usually fixed.

Lastly, the APR is updated each month, and based on the market, your APR can change on a monthly basis.

Credit Score

It's impossible to talk about credit cards without touching on the concept of credit score. In this section, I'll review the key things you should know about a credit score, but if you're looking for more detail I recommend visiting the Consumer Financial Protection Bureau's website (consumerfinance. gov) or myFICO.com.[1] These websites have in-depth coverage of credit reporting as well as many other consumer finance topics.

Your credit score is a number based on your financial history that indicates your creditworthiness (i.e., how likely you are to pay back any borrowings on time). This score ranges from 300 to 850 and is used by banks to determine how much risk premium to include in your interest rate. This applies to every type of borrowing, including credit cards, car loans, mortgages, and student loans, and the lower your score, the higher your risk premium will be. If your credit score is too low, the bank may not offer you a loan at all. Your credit score is calculated by consumer reporting agencies (the big three are Equifax, Experian, and TransUnion) and based on your *credit report*. Your credit report includes the following five pieces of information, which the consumer reporting agencies use to calculate your credit score:

1. Payment History: This shows whether you have paid your bills on time. Any late or missed payments will negatively impact your credit score. One common misconception is that you need to keep an outstanding balance on your credit card to build your credit score. This is incorrect. It's perfectly fine to pay your balance off in full every month. The important thing is to use your credit card with some degree of frequency and maintain a payment history. What the reporting agencies are looking for is that you are responsible enough to use your card and pay your bills on time. The agencies need data to support this, and if you haven't used your card, even though you don't have any late or missed payments, the reporting agency can't assess how risky you are as a borrower and will in turn lower your credit score.

2. Debt Outstanding: This metric looks at how much debt you have in total and your credit utilization. For total debt outstanding there's no hard-and-fast rule, as each person's financial situation has to be looked at individually, but the idea is you should keep your debt manageable. Credit utilization is the ratio of the outstanding balance on your *revolving accounts* (i.e., credit cards or lines of credit from a bank) to your total available credit. Generally, using above 30% of your total available credit will negatively impact your credit score. For example, if the combined limit for your credit cards is $10,000 and your balance is more than $3,000 (i.e., 30% of $10,000) then this may negatively impact your credit score.

3. Length of Credit History: The reporting agencies need a certain amount of data to accurately assess the likeliness you will pay back any borrowing and pay it back on time. A short credit history (which means less data for the rating agency) will lower your credit score.

4. Credit Mix: This records the types of credit you have, such as credit card, car loan, mortgage, or student loan. Being in good standing on many types of loans shows the agencies you are able to manage your debts well and will improve your credit score.

5. New Credit: Opening new accounts or applying for new credit, especially if done right before you apply for a loan, often indicates financial difficulty and therefore can negatively impact your credit score.

Maintaining a good credit score is a very important financial decision. Your credit score will materially impact not only your ability to get a loan, but also the interest rate you pay. Therefore, it is important to build good credit history (i.e., paying your bills on time and keeping your debt manageable) early on, and credit cards are a great way to do this. As a credit card is typically the first opportunity most consumers will have to borrow money, an effective way to build credit history is to get a credit card as soon as you turn 18, make small charges, and pay the card off in full each month. This not only establishes good credit history, but will also keep you from paying any interest on the charges.

Conclusion

Reading the fine print, although tedious, is a critical step in your financial due diligence. This chapter is not meant to be, nor can it be, all encompassing, as banks are always coming up with new finance terms and ways to charge interest. Whether purposeful or not, these terms are confusing, and not being able to navigate how your interest and fees are calculated can cost you a lot of money. My intent with this book is not to tell you what to do, but I HIGHLY recommend paying off your credit card every month.

4

PURCHASING A CAR

I t's basic human nature to want a nice car, and a car is usually one of the first major purchases anyone makes. The shine of the paint and the smell of new leather are really intoxicating, and the actual purchase process is highly emotional. Unfortunately, emotions and finance do not go well together. What I hope to do in this chapter is shed some light on the true cost of vehicle ownership and help you take emotion out of the decision-making process and replace it with some solid financial logic.

New vs. Used

The first decision you have to make is whether to buy new or used. Purchasing a new car is more expensive. What you get in return for the extra cost is the knowledge the car is in proper working order and comes with a factory warranty. Purchasing used has the potential for significant cost savings, as new car values can drop by 20% to 40% after the first three years of ownership. However, buyers beware, as you never know what problems you might encounter. This added layer of complexity means you need to do significant due diligence, such as taking the car to a trusted mechanic for a thorough inspection, before you purchase. If you don't do your due diligence, the amount of time and money you spend at the mechanic can easily outweigh any cost savings compared with the new car price. There is no right or wrong answer, and the choice depends on what you value more: a warranty and peace of mind knowing the car is in working order or potential cost savings.

Comparing the Cost Difference

Imagine the following scenario. You arrive at the local car dealership and after a bit of looking around, you find yourself torn. "Should I get the Toyota or the Lexus?" The sticker price difference is $10,000. At this point you are emotional, and deep down you are trying to justify spending the extra money. You decide to buy used, so you figure you've checked the frugality box, and ultimately you go with the Lexus. An extra $10,000 is a small price to pay for the joy of getting some nice wheels, right? But is the additional cost of ownership really only $10,000? The answer is no, and next we will look at how to calculate the actual cost difference.

In this chapter, we will do the following:

1. Compare the costs of two vehicles
2. Calculate the future value of cost savings over the ownership period

Comparing the Costs

The key here is to look beyond just the initial purchase price and fully incorporate all the additional costs. The analysis in this example can be replicated for any kind of financial comparison and does not need to be limited to the assumptions used below. Although the costs may change over time, to keep the example straightforward, I assume the additional ownership costs remain flat during the ownership period.

Let's make the following assumptions:

Price: The Lexus price is $10,000 more than the Toyota price

Ownership Period: 10 years

Fuel: Additional $442/year for the Lexus (17 * $0.50 * 52 = $442):

- Gas tank holds 17 gallons in both cars
- Lexus takes premium gasoline and Toyota takes regular
- Additional cost for premium vs. regular is $0.50/gallon
- You fill gas once per week, or 52 times per year

Maintenance/Parts Costs: An additional $500/year for the Lexus

Insurance: An additional $600/year for the Lexus

I have summarized the above assumptions in Exhibit 4.1.

Exhibit 4.1 Toyota vs. Lexus Yearly Cost Difference

Gas	$442
Maintenance	$500
Insurance	$600
Additional Yearly Cost of Ownership	$1,542

In addition to the initial difference in purchase price of $10,000, the Lexus will cost an estimated $1,542 per year more than the Toyota to own.

Calculating the Future Value

To understand the full impact, let's assume that you purchased the Toyota and invested the savings ($10,000 on the day you bought the car and $1,542 every year after that) over the 10 years of ownership. Let's also assume you can get a 6% return on any money you invest. We can estimate how much this will accumulate to in 10 years by using the *compound interest* formula to calculate the future value of each investment. As an example, let's look at the initial investment of $10,000. The formula and inputs are as follows:

Formula:

$$Principal * (1 + Interest\ Rate)^{Number\ of\ Periods}$$

Inputs:

Principal: $10,000
Interest Rate: 6%
Periods: 10

Calculation:

$$\$10,000 * (1 + 0.06)^{10} = \$10,000 * 1.791 = \$17,908$$

$10,000 invested at a 6% return will grow to $17,908 in 10 years. Next, we need to account for the $1,542 you will save each year. To get the future value of each of those investments you need to perform the compound interest calculation 10 more times. See the "Lexus vs. Toyota" tab in the accompanying Excel for the data table in Exhibit 4.2.

Exhibit 4.2 Detailed Value Calculations of Yearly Investments

	Time of Purchase	End of Year 1	End of Year 2	End of Year 3		End of Year 8	End of Year 9	End of Year 10	Value of Investment After 10 Years
Amounts you will invest	$10,000	$1,542	$1,542	$1,542		$1,542	$1,542	$1,542	
Compound Interest Formula	10,000*1.06^10	1,542*1.06^9	1,542*1.06^8	1,542*1.06^7	....	1,542*1.06^2	1,542*1.06^1	1,542*1.06^0	
FV of Investment	$17,908	$2,605	$2,458	$2,319		$1,733	$1,635	$1,542	$38,233

As you can see from these calculations, if you invest the savings from not purchasing the Lexus, after 10 years, it will grow to just over $38,000. This is the true additional cost of ownership for the Lexus. Think of all the things you could do with an extra $38,000. That sounds like a nice house down payment to me!

This is just an estimate; in reality, actual returns will never be exactly the same percentage every year. Returns will be higher or lower in any given year, and the order of returns will also impact how much your savings grow.

In conclusion, I hope you take away two things from this chapter: the first is an increased understanding of how to use the compound interest calculations, and the second is how to construct an objective evaluation that uses data for decision making and not emotions.

5

CHOOSING THE RIGHT CAREER

Work and Reality

I cringe whenever I hear people ask kids, "What do you want to be when you grow up?" The problem with this question is that most kids will base their answer on an activity they like. For example, they might say, "An actor." What they don't know is that only 10% of people can make a living in film or TV.[2] In other words, your chance of success is EXTREMELY small. What people should really be asking if they want this sort of answer is, "If you didn't have to worry about money, what would you like to do?" However, not having to worry about money does not align with reality for most of us. What we should do instead is manage expectations about work from the beginning. It is called "work" for a reason, because for most of us, if we didn't need the money, would do something else with our time. The best way to approach looking for a job is to think logically about which job will give you the highest return on time invested. If that aligns with an activity you like to do, then all the better, but the reality is it likely won't. The reality for most people is they find a job they don't mind doing, but don't particularly love either. So I'm not saying you should dread getting out of bed every day, but approaching a career from the perspective of "What do I like to do?" will likely not set you up for maximum financial success.

Choosing a Profession

Most people don't think about choosing an industry or profession as a financial decision. However, this is an extremely important decision that will have profound financial impacts for the rest of your life. For example, someone who is a good, hard-working employee in a growing industry will likely have a challenging, dynamic, and lucrative career. But that same person in a declining industry – the coal industry, for example – will likely struggle to see career opportunities and, more importantly, salary growth. So it's important to put a lot of thought into your career choice. In this chapter, I'll show you how to estimate the lifetime earnings of different professions and hopefully take some of the emotion out of the decision-making process.

Exhibit 5.1 provides information for a sample of careers. The following list describes each element in the data table:

- Years of School: Shows how many years of school you will likely need. This is not set in stone and will depend on the school you attend and/or whether you decide to go to graduate school or get additional certifications to improve your job prospects.

- Tuition & Fees of 4-Year Degree: This represents the cost range for four years of university tuition and fees, excluding room and board. According to <u>U.S. News and World Report,</u>[3] the typical cost of tuition and fees for ranked schools for the 2020–21 academic year was roughly $10,000 to $35,000. These costs vary depending on where you live (particularly if that is outside the United States), whether you get a scholarship, and so on. Remember, this is just a benchmark; the idea is not to be rigid about what costs to use, but to show you how to set up the analysis. As the cost of tuition can vary greatly, I have used the same range for each profession. I did not factor in graduate school costs as there are too many variables to come up with an accurate estimate.

- Hours per Week: This shows the range of hours per week you are likely to work in a specific profession.

- 2019 Yearly Salary Range: This data is from the <u>U.S. Bureau of Labor Statistics Occupational Outlook Handbook</u>[4] and shows what the bottom 10%, median, and top 10% of earners make for each profession. Again, the idea is not to be prescriptive about what numbers to use. If you work outside the United States or have different estimates based on your research, that's fine. All I'm trying to do is show you how to think through your choices.

- Estimated $/Hour Range: For each profession this shows the estimated earnings as a $/hour rate based on 48 weeks of work per year (52 – 4, which includes two weeks of vacation and two weeks of national/state holidays) for the bottom 10% and top 10% of earners. For teachers, the rate is calculated on 40 weeks per year to adjust for 12 weeks of summer and winter vacation (i.e., 52 – 12).

- Earnings Potential: Those who work at large corporations, which is typical for financial analysts, lawyers, and computer programmers, have potential to become executive management. Executive earnings are not limited by a specific profession, and earnings potential is essentially uncapped.

There is no way to put together an exhaustive list of careers. For any job you're interested in, I recommend identifying potential employers and looking at the careers portion of their website. This will give you an idea of the universities they recruit from, degree requirements, etc. There are also websites, such as Glassdoor.com, where employees anonymously give salary information and company reviews; you can use such sites to get a much better idea of the salary by company, job, and location. Lastly, in order to keep the focus manageable, I purposely did not include estimates for non-salary-based benefits. Non-salary benefits can be monetary, such as a higher company match to a retirement plan or a transportation allowance, or non-monetary, such as access to the company suite for professional sporting events or access to the company's services at a reduced cost (e.g., discounted flight tickets for airline employees). This is not to say that non-salary benefits should not be considered, but they need to be evaluated on a career-by-career and company-by-company basis, and the degree of variability is too high to capture in this analysis.

Exhibit 5.1 Sample Career Information

Career	Years of School		Tuition & Fees of 4 Year Degree	Hours Per Week	2019 Yearly Salary Range			Estimated $/Hour Range*	Earnings Potential
					Bottom 10%	Median	Top 10%		
Financial Analysts	4-6	Requires an undergraduate and/or masters degree for most Fortune 500 companies. An MBA, Masters in Accounting or CPA also common.	$40,000 - $120,000	40 - 60	$47,230	$81,590	$156,150	$25 - $54	$1,000,000 +
Pharmacist	7-8	Requires post graduate school of 3-4 years to earn a Doctor of Pharmacy.	$40,000 - $120,000	40 - 50	$88,400	$128,090	$162,900	$46 - $68	
High School Teacher	4	Requires a 4 year college degree, teaching license and will most likely need to major in the subject you teach.	$40,000 - $120,000	40 - 60	$40,540	$61,660	$99,660	$25 - $42	
Dentist	8	Requires 4 year under graduate degree (including Dental School prerequisite classes) and 4 years of Dental School to earn your DDS (Doctor of Dental Surgery).	$40,000 - $120,000	35 - 50	$79,670	$159,200	$208,000	$47 - $87	
Lawyer	7	Requires undergrad & law degree (3 years of law school) and must pass bar exam.	$40,000 - $120,000	40 - 60	$59,670	$122,960	$208,000	$31 - $72	$1,000,000 +
Computer Programmer	4	Requires a 4 year degree in Computer Science and will likely need to become certified in specific computer language.	$40,000 - $120,000	40 - 60	$50,150	$86,550	$140,250	$26 - $49	$1,000,000 +
Plumber	1< year	Requires a High School degree to start working. You must then complete an apprenticeship for 4-5 years, after which you pass an exam to become licensed.	N/A - N/A	40 - 50	$44,480	$71,550	$124,450	$23 - $52	

*Estimated $/Hour Range Assumes two weeks vacation per year (i.e. 50 weeks of work)

*Estimated $/Hour Range for teachers assumes 12 weeks of summer & winter break per year (i.e. 40 weeks of work)

Note: See the "Picking a Career" tab in the accompanying Excel for this data table.

To see how to use the data table, let's compare a plumber and a pharmacist.

Plumber: This profession does not require a college degree. Typically, becoming a plumber requires an apprenticeship, followed by a test upon completion to become certified. You can start earning income almost immediately as the classroom preparation is minimal and most of the training is on the job. There is a wide range for salaries ($44,000 to $124,000), and the salary will likely get closer to the higher end as you gain more experience. However, unlike most 9–5 jobs, plumbers often get calls during odd hours, at night, and on weekends to handle emergencies.

Pharmacist: This profession requires a minimum four-year college degree and three or four years of pharmacy school to earn a Doctor of Pharmacy degree. College costs and the amount of debt upon graduation will vary greatly, depending on where you go to school, whether you receive financial aid, and other factors. However, as you have to attend a minimum of seven years of school, you are likely to come out with substantial debt. Earnings can have a significant degree of variability ($88,000 to $128,000). The $/hour rate also varies widely. Earnings potential is likely capped at the higher end of the salary range as pharmacists typically stay within their profession and do not move to executive management. If the executive management path is chosen, regardless of the corporation, it is very difficult and will require many long days and nights at the office.

Let's take these two examples a step further and try to quantify the lifetime earnings of a plumber and a pharmacist. To do this we will calculate the after-tax *present value* (i.e., value of future earnings in today's dollars) of the estimated net lifetime earnings (i.e., earnings minus debt payments) for each profession.

We'll start with the plumber and make the following assumptions:

Assumptions:

Education Loan: $0 (as the training is mostly on the job, there are no costs for school)

Work Years: 40 *periods* (start work on 18th birthday, assumed to fall on January 1, and retire at the end of the year age 57)

Inflation rate: 3% (the amount we discount future earnings by to get them in today's dollars; this will be compounded yearly)

Wage Inflation: 2% (the amount salary will increase annually over working years)

Starting Wage: $44,480 (the bottom 10% of the estimated yearly salary range)

Effective Tax Rate: 15% (estimated average tax rate paid on all earnings. The effective tax rate for the starting salary is around 15%, and as both the salary and tax brackets will grow in line with *inflation*, we use this rate for the entire time frame. See the "PV of Future Earnings" tab in the accompanying Excel for detailed tax brackets)

Now we can use the above assumptions to calculate the after-tax present value of each year's future earnings. The formula and inputs are as follows:

Formula:

> (Full-Year Earnings – Taxes – Student Debt Repayment)/*Discount rate*

As the calculation needs to be done separately for each year (i.e., 40 calculations), this is best tackled in Excel. However, I will use years 1 and 2 as an example to break down the calculations.

Year 1 (Age 18)

Inputs:

> Earnings: $44,480 (the starting wage from the assumptions above)
>
> Taxes: –$6,672 (tax rate of 15% applied to earnings of $44,480 [$44,480 * 15%]; this is negative because taxes are subtracted from earnings)
>
> Student Debt Repayment: $0 (because the plumber has no debt)
>
> Discount Rate: $1.03^1 = (1 + \text{Inflation Rate})^{\text{Number of Periods}}$
>
>> This is the factor by which we reduce future earnings. The number of periods represents how many years you are away from today, and as the number of periods grows, so will the discount rate.

Calculation:

> Net Earnings: $44,480 – $6,672 = $37,808
>
> Present Value of After-Tax Earnings: $37,808/1.03 = $36,707
>
>> The present value calculation is the opposite of the future value calculation covered in Chapter 4 ("Purchasing a Car"). Instead of multiplying today's dollars by an interest rate factor to get the future value, we divide future dollars using a discount rate (i.e., we reduce future earnings to adjust for inflation) to get the money in today's value.

Year 2 (Age 19)

Inputs:

> Earnings: $45,370 (starting wage from year 1 inflated by 2% [$44,480 * 1.02])
>
> Taxes: –$6,805 (tax rate of 15% applied to earnings of $45,370 [$45,370 * 15%]; this is negative because taxes are subtracted from earnings)
>
> Student Debt Repayment: $0 (because the plumber has no debt)
>
> Discount Rate: $1.0609 = 1.03^2 = (1 + \text{Inflation Rate})^{\text{Number of Periods}}$

Calculation:

> Net Earnings: $45,370 – $6,805 = $38,564
>
> Present Value of After-Tax Earnings: $38,564/1.0609 = $36,350

As an aside, notice the present value of the after-tax earnings in year 2 is actually less than in year 1 ($36,350 vs. $36,707). This is because inflation rose faster than the salary (3% vs. 2%). It is important to keep an eye on this, because even if your salary increases every year, if it increases by less than inflation, then your salary in real terms is actually reduced.

Lastly, for each subsequent period (i.e., 38 more times), perform the same calculations as above and sum the after-tax present value of each year's earnings to get a present value of total lifetime earnings for the plumber of $1,221,616.

These calculations are summarized in Exhibit 5.2 and can be found in detail on the "PV of Future Earnings" tab in the accompanying Excel.

Exhibit 5.2 Plumber Lifetime Earnings Summary

Assumptions										
Education Loan	$0			**Year 1**	**Year 2**	**Year 3**		**Year 28**	**Year 29**	**Year 30**
Work Years	40		Age at Beginning of Year	18	19	20		55	56	57
Inflation Rate	3.00%		Full Year Earnings	$44,480	$45,370	$46,277		$92,549	$94,400	$96,228
Wage Inflation	2.00%		Taxes	($6,672)	($6,805)	($6,942)		($13,133)	($14,160)	($14,433)
Starting Wage	$44,480		Student Debt Repayment	$0	$0	$0		$0	$0	$0
Effective tax rate	15.00%		Net Earnings	$37,808	$38,564	$39,335		$78,667	$80,240	$81,845
Present Value of Total After-Tax Lifetime Earnings	1,221,616		Discount Rate Formula	1.03^1	1.03^2	1.03^3		1.03^38	1.03^39	1.03^40
			Discount Rate	1.0300	1.0609	1.0927		3.0748	3.1670	3.2620
			Present Value of After Tax Earnings	*$36,707*	*$36,350*	*$35,998*		*$25,584*	*$25,336*	*$25,090*

Next, let's calculate the after-tax present value (i.e., value of future earnings in today's dollars) of the estimated net lifetime earnings (i.e., earnings minus debt payments) for the pharmacist.

Assumptions:

Education Loan: $200,000, comprising:

Undergraduate tuition, fees, room & board: $20,000 per year (4 * $20,000) = $80,000

Pharmacy School tuition, fees, room & board: $30,000 per year (4 * $30,000) = $120,000
This is just an example, and there are many things you could do to mitigate these costs. You could work part time to pay for living costs, get scholarships, live at home, go to a cheaper school, etc.

Also, there will be *accrued interest* while you are in school because you will not start paying back the loan immediately (i.e., you will be charged *interest* ever year and that interest will be added to the outstanding balance until you start paying down the loan). Therefore, the total amount owed when you graduate will be more than you originally borrowed. For ease of this example, I am not accounting for this, but if you wanted to get a more accurate estimate you would need to factor accrued interest into your payback amount.

Tuition & Fees Payback: $10,000 per year for 30 years

> Although you can definitely pay your loans off faster, according to the <u>Department of Education Federal Student Aid Office</u>[5], the maximum repayment period under the standard repayment plan for a student loan over $60,000 is 30 years. So we'll assume the loans are paid off over 30 years and payments are $10,000 per year. The exact amount of payback will depend on the type of loan, the interest rate, and your willingness to make additional payments. Again, for ease of this example I am using a flat $10,000 per year.

Work Years: 32 periods (start work on 26th birthday, assumed to fall on January 1, and retire at the end of the year age 57)

Inflation: 3% (the amount we will discount future earnings by to get them in today's dollars; this will be compounded yearly)

Wage Inflation: 2%

Starting Wage: $88,400 (this is the bottom 10% of the estimated yearly salary range)

Effective Tax Rate: 20% (estimated average tax rate paid on all earnings. As the earnings are higher for the pharmacist, the effective tax rate is around 20%. Both the salary and tax brackets will grow in line with inflation, so we use this rate for the entire time frame. See the "PV of Future Earnings" tab in the accompanying Excel for detailed tax brackets)

Similar to the previous example, we will use the above assumptions to calculate the after-tax present value of each year's future earnings. Let's break the calculations up into three periods: years 1–8 (when the pharmacist is still in school), years 9–38 (the loan payback period), and years 39–40 (after loan payback through to retirement).

Years 1–8
In years 1–8 there are no earnings as the pharmacist is still in school and not working, so no calculations are necessary.

Years 9–38
The calculation needs to be done separately for each year (i.e., 30 calculations), so this exercise is best tackled in Excel. However, I will use years 9 and 10 as examples to break down the calculations.

Year 9
Inputs:

Future Earnings: $88,400 (the starting wage from the assumptions above)

Taxes: –$17,680 (tax rate of 20% applied to earnings of $88,400 [$88,400 * 20%]; this is negative because taxes are subtracted from earnings)

Student Debt Repayment: –$10,000

Discount Rate: $1.03^9 = (1 + \text{Inflation Rate})^{\text{Number of Periods}}$

> This is the factor by which we reduce future earnings. The number of periods represents how many years you are away from today, and as the number of periods grows, so will the discount rate. In this case, because year 9 is the first full year of work for the pharmacist, the number of periods is 9.

Calculation:

Net Earnings: $88,400 − $17,680 − $10,000 = $60,720

Present Value of After-Tax Earnings: $60,720/1.3048 = $46,537

The present value calculation is the opposite of the future value calculation covered in Chapter 4. Instead of multiplying today's dollars to get the future value, we divide future dollars using a discount rate (i.e., reduce future earnings to adjust for inflation) to get the money in today's value.

Year 10

Inputs:

Future Earnings: $90,168 (the starting wage from year 9 inflated by 2% [$88,400 * 1.02])

Taxes: −$18,034 (tax rate of 20% applied to earnings of $90,168 [$90,168 * 20%]; this is negative because taxes are subtracted from earnings)

Student Debt Repayment: −$10,000

Discount Rate: $1.03^{10} = (1 + \text{Inflation Rate})^{\text{Number of Periods}}$

Calculation:

Net Earnings: $90,168 − $18,034 − $10,000 = $62,134

Present Value of After-Tax Earnings: $62,134/1.3439 = $46,234

Again, notice the present value of the after-tax earnings in year 10 is actually less than in year 9 ($46,234 vs. $46,537). This is because inflation rose faster than the salary (3% vs. 2%).

This calculation must be done 28 more times, and the present value for this period will total to $1,261,844. A summary of the calculations is provided in Exhibit 5.3 and in the accompanying Excel.

Exhibit 5.3 Pharmacist Earnings Summary Years 9–38

	Year 9	Year 10	Year 11		Year 36	Year 37	Year 38
Age at Beginning of Year	26	27	28		53	54	55
Full Year Earnings	$88,400	$90,168	$91,971		$150,889	$153,907	$156,985
Taxes	($17,680)	($18,034)	($18,394)		($30,178)	($30,781)	($31,397)
Student Debt Repayment	($10,000)	($10,000)	($10,000)	......	($10,000)	($10,000)	($10,000)
Net Earnings	$60,720	$62,134	$63,577		$110,711	$113,125	$115,588
Discount Rate Formula	1.03^9	1.03^10	1.03^11		1.03^36	1.03^37	1.03^35
Discount Rate	1.3048	1.3439	1.3842		2.8983	2.9852	3.0748
Present Value of After Tax Earnings	$46,537	$46,234	$45,929		$38,199	$37,895	$37,592

Years 39–40

The only difference during this period is that there is no student debt to deduct; otherwise, the calculations are the same as above. As such, I will not go through the calculations again and have provided a summary in Exhibit 5.4. Detailed calculations can be found on the "PV of Future Earnings" tab in the accompanying Excel.

Exhibit 5.4 Pharmacist Earnings Summary Years 39–40

	Year 39	Year 40
Age at Beginning of Year	56	57
Full Year Earnings	$160,124	$163,327
Taxes	($32,025)	($32,665)
Student Debt Repayment	$0	$0
Net Earnings	$128,099	$130,661
Discount Rate Formula	1.03^39	1.03^40
Discount Rate	3.1670	3.2620
Present Value of After Tax Earnings	$40,448	$40,055
Present Value Total After-Tax Earnings for Years 39-40	$80,503	

The last step is to sum the after-tax present values for each of the three periods ($0 + $1,261,844 + $80,503) to get the lifetime earnings in today's dollars, which is $1,342,347. This is greater than the figure we calculated for the plumber by $120,731 ($1,342,347 − $1,221,616). It is in year 31 that the present value of the pharmacist's total earnings overtakes the present value of the plumber's total earnings (i.e., when the pharmacist is 48 years old). Even though the pharmacist's salary is significantly more than the plumber's, the pharmacist has substantial student loans to pay back and starts working eight years after the plumber. Thus, the present value of the pharmacist's earnings is significantly diminished, and this is why it takes so long to overtake the plumber. The debt in particular is holding the pharmacist back, and if the cost of education can be lowered, the economics of the pharmacy career improve significantly.

In this comparison the net present value of lifetime earnings for the two professions is pretty similar (the pharmacist's total earnings are only $120,731 more), so there is no strong financial case to choose one over the other. The takeaway is not that one career is better than the other, but the thought process to evaluate the financial implications of different career choices in a systematic way so you can decide for yourself what's best.

Now that you understand how to run the numbers, you can combine this knowledge with your personal preferences for a more objective evaluation of the trade-offs of different careers.

6

PAYING OFF STUDENT LOANS

This chapter will be short, as it is fairly straightforward. When you have more than one loan, student or other, you should pay off the loans in descending order of their *interest rates* (i.e., start with the highest interest rate loan first and work your way down to the loan with the lowest interest rate). This is the correct action to take from a purely financial perspective, and if this approach is followed, you will pay the least amount of *interest* on your loans.

However, you have to consider your emotions and how they impact your financial judgement. We are human beings, not robots, and for some people this approach may not work. For some it is more important to see a loan paid off, even if it is not the highest interest rate loan, so they can maintain motivation. Dave Ramsey has coined the term the "Debt Snowball Method" to describe the second approach.[6] Ultimately you must decide which approach is right for you, but the key is to develop a plan you can stick to and get the money paid back as soon as possible.

7

DEFINED CONTRIBUTION PLANS

Congratulations, you've landed a job. You will now become an active member of the labor force, get to pay your fair share of taxes, and begin the climb up the corporate ladder. If all this doesn't excite you enough, there is also the mountain of paperwork you will have to complete on your first day of work. Part of that paperwork is usually a form to opt in to some kind of *defined contribution plan*. A defined contribution plan is an employer-offered retirement plan where employees contribute a percentage of their salary into a retirement account. Typically, the account is *tax-deferred* -- a portion of the employee contribution is matched by the employer, and the funds are restricted for some period of time.

In the United States, common defined contribution plans include the *401(k)*, 403(b), and thrift savings plan. These plans share the following characteristics:

Tax Deferral: Employees contribute a portion of their pre-tax salary and the account is allowed to grow tax-free until the funds are withdrawn. Except under special circumstances, funds are not to be withdrawn before age 59½ without penalty. When funds are withdrawn, taxes are paid at the employee's ordinary income tax rate.

Contribution Limit: As of 2020, for employees under 50 years old, the yearly contribution limit was $19,500.

The main difference in these plans is the type of institution that offers the plan. A 401(k) is offered by for-profit entities, a 403(b) is offered by public schools/nonprofits, and a thrift savings plan is offered by the U.S. government.[7] For more details on various plans, I recommend visiting the retirement plans section of the <u>Internal Revenue Service</u>[8] website or <u>CNN Money's Ultimate Guide to Retirement</u>.[9]

In this chapter, we will do the following:

1. Evaluate the benefits of tax deferral
2. Discuss how to choose an *investment fund*:
    a. Money market, bonds, and stocks
    b. *Index* vs. *actively managed funds*

3. Calculate the impact of management fees
4. Discuss the differences between a 401(k), Roth 401(k), IRA, and Roth IRA and when to choose a regular or a Roth account
5. Discuss how much of your pay you should contribute to an employer-sponsored plan

Evaluating the Benefits of Tax Deferral

Tax-deferred accounts are a truly powerful way to grow your savings. In a tax-deferred account you invest money pre-tax (i.e., before you pay any taxes) and the money grows tax free as long as it is not withdrawn from the account. This significantly increases the future value of your money because not only do you not have to pay taxes on the initial investment amount, but any gains can also grow tax free.

Let's look at an example. Say you are 25 years old and have $10,000 of pre-tax income to invest. Your options are to invest in your employer's defined contribution plan or pay taxes and invest the money at your local bank. Assume both investments will pay you a 6% yearly return and you will re-invest all returns until retirement at age 60. Let's first look at what happens if you invest in the employer tax-deferred plan.

See the "Benefits of Tax Deferral" tab in the accompanying Excel file for detailed calculations.

The formula and inputs are as follows:
Formula:

$$Principal * (1 + Interest\ Rate)^{Number\ of\ Periods} * (1 - Tax\ Rate)$$

Inputs:

Principal:	$10,000
Interest Rate:	6%
Periods:	35
Retirement Tax Rate:	15%

Calculation:
Let's break the formula into two steps. The first step is to calculate the future value of the investment before tax. This is just the *compound interest* formula:

$$\$10,000 * (1 + 0.06)^{35} = \$10,000 * 7.686 = \$76,861$$

Next we apply taxes. Because the investment has been growing tax free for 35 years, when you withdraw the funds you must pay tax on the entire amount at your ordinary income tax rate, which we assume is 15%.

$$\$76,861 * (1 - Tax\ Rate) = \$76,861 * 0.85 = \$65,332$$

After 35 years your money will grow from $10,000 to $65,332, or by roughly six times.

Now let's take a look at what will happen if you instead decide to invest the money at your local bank. We assume the bank has only a normal investment account (i.e., not tax deferred) and you have to pay ordinary income taxes on the $10,000 before you can invest it. In addition, you will have to pay income tax each year on any gains you receive from the investment.

The formula and inputs are as follows:
Formula:

{Principal * (1 − Tax Rate)} * (1 + {Interest Rate * (1 − Tax Rate)})$^{\text{Number of Periods}}$

Inputs:

Principal:	$10,000
Interest Rate:	6%
Periods:	35
Current Tax Rate:	15%

Notice the formula changed in two ways. First, you have to pay taxes immediately on the initial $10,000 investment. Assume the $10,000 is a bonus you received from your job and, as with any other salary, the company withholds federal, state, and payroll taxes from that money. So your tax rate of 15% is applied to the principal, which reduces your initial investment to $8,500:

$10,000 * (1 − 0.15) = $10,000 * 0.85 = $8,500

Next the tax rate is applied again to your interest rate. This is because each year, as you make a return on your investment, you have to pay some of that return to the government as taxes. This effectively lowers your return. The following calculation shows by how much the return is lowered:

Interest Rate * (1 − Tax Rate) = 6.0% * (1 − 0.15) = 5.1%

Because of taxes, your return is lowered each year to 5.1%. If you put the entire formula together the calculations are as follows:

$8,500 * (1 + 0.051)^{35} = $8,500 * 5.703 = $48,475

So due to the *tax drag* (i.e., additional taxes paid over the life of the investment), your investment is reduced by $16,857 ($48,475 vs. $65,332).

Choosing an Investment Fund

After doing the above calculations, you realize it's much more beneficial to use your company's defined contribution plan. However, your employer has a large selection of funds, and you are confused as to which one is best.

Money Market, Bonds, and Stocks

Typically, the investment choices will be broken into money market, bonds, and stock funds. What follows is a basic summary of each:

Money Market Fund: Puts your money in highly *liquid* (i.e., easily convertible into cash) investments. These investments have the lowest risk and lowest return and should be used as a place to park your cash. However, be warned: even though the name has the word "money" in it, money market funds are not cash. Although rare, if there is a severe market crash, the value of these investments can and does decline.

Bond Fund: Bonds are loans made by an investor to a borrower where the borrower usually pays a fixed payment over the life of the loan. These are a great source of steady income, and the range of options offers something for every investor risk preference. From least to most risky, bond options range from government-issued bonds, (which are considered to be risk-free because the government literally has a money printing press), investment-grade corporate bonds (issued by the most creditworthy companies), all the way to junk bonds (issued by the least creditworthy companies). Government bonds (least risky) offer the lowest return, while junk bonds (most risky) offer the highest, and investors have options across the range of creditworthiness to choose bonds based on whatever their needs and risk preferences are. The bond market is vast. Websites such as moodys.com and spglobal.com are great resources to learn more.

Stock Fund: Stocks represent partial ownership in companies and entitle you to a portion of a company's assets and profits. Unlike bond investments, where a periodic fixed payment is received, owners of company stock are compensated in two ways:

1. Capital Appreciation (i.e., the increase in stock price): As the company makes more money, its value will increase and the stockholders will be able to sell the stock to other investors for a higher price.
2. Dividends: Dividends are when a company pays out a portion of its earnings to the stockholders.

Stock funds come in almost infinite varieties, and there are options for all investor preferences. Here is a brief summary of common funds types:

Growth: Focuses on companies that are growing faster than average for their industry. These stocks typically do not pay a dividend, and profit is made through capital appreciation.

Value: Includes companies that are undervalued compared with their peers. These companies typically pay a dividend, and profits are made via dividend income and/or capital appreciation.

Sector: Concentrates on a specific sector of the economy, such as technology, energy, or pharmaceuticals.

Market Capitalization: Holds stocks in companies of a certain size and is typically broken up into small, medium, and large capitalization funds.

Region: Contains stocks of companies in a particular country or region of the world (United States, Europe, Latin America, China, etc.)

Target Date: A combination of money market, bonds, and stocks. Based on your target retirement date, these funds automatically shift the allocation between money market, bonds, and stocks to generate maximum return with the appropriate level of risk as you age. As bonds provide steady income, the allocation is typically shifted more toward bonds as you get closer to retirement.

For more information on the different types of money market, bond, and stock funds, I recommend CNN Money's Ultimate Guide to Retirement.[9]

Lastly, you should seek advice from an investment professional to help you decide which specific fund or combination of funds is right for you. (This is discussed further in Chapter 11, "Investing for Retirement.")

Actively Managed vs. Index Funds

Both bonds and stocks can be purchased directly by an individual or via an investment fund. Most companies, however, will not allow employees to select individual bonds or stocks for their defined contribution plans and employees must invest via investment funds. The reason for using the investment fund option is that most individuals lack the time and technical expertise to pick specific bonds or stocks and build a diversified portfolio. Investment funds allow people to pool their money, which gives investors access to more investment opportunities and allows them to have a professional management team look after the investments.

Investment funds typically come in two types: active and index. In an actively managed fund, management uses a proprietary strategy to earn a higher return. Management fees are usually higher as you are paying for the managers' skill and the potential for higher returns. Actively managed funds come in all shapes and sizes, and just about any combination of growth, value, sector, region, etc. is available.

Index funds (also known as passive funds) track the performance of an index (a theoretical portfolio of investments in some segment of the financial market). You cannot invest directly in an index and in most cases have to invest in an index fund that will purchase the stocks or bonds to replicate the index. The best known index funds are the S&P 500 Index (which is an index of the 500 largest companies in the United States and is generally accepted as a representation of the U.S. market as a whole) and the Dow Jones Industrial Average (which tracks the 30 largest companies in the United States). However, there are indexes for most any combination of growth, value, sector, region, etc. An additional benefit of index funds is their low management fee. An index fund manager's only job is to mimic the index; therefore the fees are mostly administrative and as such kept to a minimum.

The Impact of Management Fees

As I mentioned in the previous section, all investment funds have management fees. Fees vary, and there is no standard; however, lower fees are always better for the investor. Typically, fees range from 0.2% (on the low end) for a large index fund to 2.5% (on the very high end) for an actively managed fund. Management fees are calculated as a percentage of *assets under management* (i.e., the value of the investment the fund is managing on the investor's behalf). Let's walk through a few examples to see how fees can impact returns.

Assume you are choosing between two funds that are offered via your employer's defined contribution plan. One is a passively managed S&P 500 index fund, and the other is an actively managed fund. Let's also assume the management fees (you may also see these referred to as the "expense ratio") are 0.2% and 2.5% respectively and that you are currently 25 years old, will invest $10,000, will make a 6% return, and will take the money out at 60 years old. First, we'll look at what happens if you invest in the actively managed fund.

The formula and inputs are as follows:
Formula:

$$(\text{Principal} * \{(1 + \text{Interest Rate}) * (1 - \text{Management Fee})\}^{\text{Number of Periods}}) * (1 - \text{Retirement Tax Rate})$$

Inputs:
>Principal: $10,000
>Interest Rate: 6%
>Management Fee: 2.5% (assume fee is charged once per year at the end of the year)
>Periods: 35
>Retirement Tax Rate: 15%

Calculation:
The formula above is a bit tricky as the management fee is applied to the entire amount invested, every year, not just the returns. Also, because this is a tax-deferred account, you don't have to pay tax on the initial investment. You pay tax only when you withdraw the money at 60 years old. Let's break the formula into steps. First, let's calculate the investment return after fees:

>$(1 + \text{Interest Rate}) * (1 - \text{Management Fee}) = 1.06 * (1 - 0.025) = 1.0335$

Next, we compound the returns for 35 years:

>$\text{Principal} * (1.0335)^{\text{Number of Periods}} = \$10,000 * (1.0335)^{35} = \$10,000 * 3.169 = \$31,686$

Lastly, we pay tax on the future amount:

>$\$31,686 * (1 - \text{Retirement Tax Rate}) = \$31,686 * (1 - 0.15) = \$26,933$

After 35 years you will end up with $26,933.

Next let's look at the same investment of $10,000 in the index fund and assume the only difference is a lower management fee of 0.2%.

The formula and inputs are as follows:
Formula:

$$(\text{Principal} * \{(1 + \text{Interest Rate}) * (1 - \text{Management Fee})\}^{\text{Number of Periods}}) * (1 - \text{Retirement Tax Rate})$$

Inputs:

    Principal: $10,000

    Interest Rate: 6%

    Management Fee: 0.2% (assume fee is charged once per year at the end of the year)

    Periods: 35

    Retirement Tax Rate: 15%

Calculation:

Again, let's break the formula into steps. First, let's calculate the investment return after fees:

    (1 + Interest Rate) * (1 − Management Fee) = 1.06 * (1 − 0.002) = 1.0579

Next, we compound the returns for 35 years:

    Principal * $(1.0579)^{\text{Number of Periods}}$ = $10,000 * $(1.0579)^{35}$ = $10,000 * 7.166 = $71,660

Lastly, we pay tax on the future amount:

    Future Value * (1 − Retirement Tax Rate) = $71,660 * (1 − 0.15) = $60,911

After 35 years you will end up with $60,911.

Even though the management fee differs by only 2.3% (2.5% − 0.2%), the impact is that you lose significant future gains ($26,933 vs. $60,911) to these additional fees in the actively managed fund.

If we take the above example a step further, assume you contribute $10,000 a year for 35 years to the plan, and compare the final after-tax values, the actively managed fund will leave you with approximately $569,000 and the index fund will leave you with $958,000. To compute the return for yearly contributions you need to run the above calculations 35 times (i.e., once for each year) and add them all together. Needless to say, I will not go into that level of detail; however, if you want to see the detailed calculations you can refer to the "Impact of Management Fees" tab in the accompanying Excel file. In summary, fees should be kept at a minimum as higher fees result in a significant drain on your investment returns.

401(k) vs. IRA and Roth 401(k) vs. Roth IRA

As mentioned at the beginning of this chapter, a 401(k), a 403(b) and a thrift savings plan are all very similar. Therefore, I will use the 401(k) as an example for the comparisons going forward.

A 401(k) is an employer-offered, tax-deferred retirement account. Funds are taken directly from your paycheck on a pre-tax basis (i.e., before you pay taxes on them) and invested in a fund of your choosing. The employee contribution limit as of 2020 was $19,500 per year if the employee was under 50 years old, and $26,000 if they were over 50 years old. At 59½ you can withdraw the money without penalty, and you pay ordinary income taxes on any amount you withdraw.

An IRA (Individual Retirement Account) is almost identical to a 401(k) except it is for people who do not have an employer-sponsored plan and has lower contribution limits (as of 2020 the limit was $6,000 per year if the person was under 50 years old, and $7,000 if they were over 50 years old). You set this account up yourself either with your local bank or with your investment broker (e.g., E-Trade, Vanguard, and Fidelity), contributions are made on a pre-tax basis, and at 59½ you can withdraw money without penalty and pay ordinary income taxes on any amount you withdraw.

A Roth 401(k) and a Roth IRA are the same as their non-Roth counterparts except that you contribute to the accounts after tax (i.e., you pay taxes on the money now). The funds then grow tax free, and when you withdraw the funds, after age 59½, any withdrawal is tax-free. This is also referred to as a tax-exempt account. Most employers will have both Roth and non-Roth options.

As an aside, for very high earners (in 2020 those filing jointly with an adjusted gross income of more than about $200,000 per year), the IRS may limit your contributions to traditional and Roth 401(k)/IRA plans. The income limits, and when and how much they apply, are quite nuanced and beyond the scope of this section. If you think your income might be above this threshold, I recommend speaking with a tax expert. For more information, in the endnotes, I have included a reference to Investopedia,[10] where you can find additional coverage of contribution limits for 401(k)/IRA plans.

Choosing between a Roth and a Non-Roth Account

The major determining factor in deciding to go with a Roth or non-Roth retirement account is your tax rate. With a regular 401(k) or IRA, you pay taxes when you withdraw the money. For most people their tax rate is lower in retirement because they are not working and have lower income. If you think you will have a lower tax rate in retirement, you should delay paying taxes and choose the traditional 401(k). If you think you will have a higher tax rate in retirement, then you should pay taxes now and take your money tax free later on (i.e., go with a Roth account). Given the intricacies of different tax regimes, you should consult with your accountant to get the best idea of what your future tax rate might be. In addition, it's prudent to consider changes in the future political landscape. It is entirely possible that a future government will change the tax laws. If you have not paid taxes on your money and the tax laws are changed (i.e., income taxes are increased), you might face a negative impact to your standard of living. So, even if you think you will have a lower tax rate in retirement, it may be wise to put something into a Roth account. I personally contribute funds to both a Roth and a non-Roth account to hedge my bets.

Let's take a look at a few examples and see how different tax rate assumptions impact the decision between a non-Roth and a Roth retirement account.

In the first example, let's assume you have $10,000 to invest for 35 years, you will earn a 6% return, your retirement tax rate is 15%, and you will invest in a non-Roth 401(k) (i.e., pre-tax account). The formula and calculation are as follows:

Formula:
  Principal * (1 + Interest Rate)$^{\text{Number of Periods}}$ * (1 − Retirement Tax Rate)

Inputs:
  Principal: $10,000
  Interest Rate: 6%
  Periods: 35
  Retirement Tax Rate: 15%

Calculation:
  $10,000 * (1 + 0.06)^{35} = $10,000 * 7.686 = $76,861
  $76,861 * (1 − 0.15) = $76,861 * 0.85 = $65,332

After 35 years, your money will grow from $10,000 to $65,332, or by roughly six times.

Now let's see how your money will grow by investing in a Roth 401(k) (i.e., after-tax account). We'll use the same assumptions as in the non-Roth example with the exception of your current tax rate, which we'll assume is 20%. The formula and calculation are as follows:

Formula:
  Principal * (1 − Current Tax Rate) * (1 + Interest Rate)$^{\text{Number of Periods}}$

Inputs:
  Principal: $10,000
  Interest Rate: 6%
  Periods: 35
  Current Tax Rate: 20%

Calculation:
  $10,000 * (1 − 0.20) = $10,000 * 0.80 = $8,000
  $8,000 * (1 + 0.06)^{35} = $8,000 * 7.686 = $61,489

After 35 years, your money will grow from $10,000 to $61,489, which is $3,843 ($61,489 vs. $65,332) less than the previous, non-Roth example. Because your current tax rate is higher (20% vs. 15%), by paying taxes now you realize a higher tax rate.

In summary, while keeping in mind the possibility of any potential future tax law changes, you should go with whatever account will allow you to realize the lowest tax rate. If you expect your current tax rate is lower than your tax rate will be in retirement, you should pay taxes now (i.e., go with a Roth account). If your retirement tax rate is expected to be lower, then you should go with a traditional (i.e., non-Roth) account.

How Much to Contribute to an Employer-Sponsored Plan

How much you need to save in a defined contribution plan will depend on many factors, such as your retirement goals, other sources of income, and returns on investments. Therefore, it is impossible for me to tell you exactly how much to save. What I can tell you is that if your employer offers a contribution match (employers will usually match up to a certain percentage of your salary or a certain dollar amount), you should always contribute enough to maximize the match.

Let's go through an example. Say your employer offers to match the contribution to your 401(k) dollar for dollar up to 3% of your salary and you make $100,000 per year. This means your employer will contribute up to an additional $3,000 to your 401(k). If you contribute 3% of your salary (i.e., $3,000), you will actually get $6,000 in your account. The additional $3,000 contributed by your employer is free money; therefore, you should always contribute enough to maximize the employer match no matter what!

8

PURCHASING A HOUSE

Congratulations, you've reached a huge financial milestone and are ready to purchase your first home. As this is likely the biggest purchase you will ever make, it's worth spending a bit of time on.

Most people think of a house as an asset, and of owning a house as an important step to economic success. While I don't disagree with this, I urge you to take your thinking a step further. I urge you to look at all assets as income producing or non-income producing. A house that you live in is a non-income-producing asset (i.e., it only costs you money). In addition to the loan repayments, there are property taxes, insurance, maintenance, Homeowners Association fees, and the innumerable trips to the hardware store for all those side projects. This all adds up, and as wonderful as a home can be, it is also a real money drain! I'm not saying owning a home is bad; you have to live somewhere, and I think anyone who desires to should be able to have a place of their own.

Just like buying a car, purchasing a home is an intensely personal and emotional decision. A new home can bring you joy and be a place to make happy memories. But there is a fine line between a home being a burden or a blessing, and you should be thoughtful about what you can realistically afford. The goal of this chapter is to help you make an informed, data-driven decision and know exactly what you're getting yourself into.

What is a Mortgage?
A *mortgage* is usually thought of as the contract you sign when getting a home loan. However, there are actually two distinct documents you sign when purchasing a home:

Promissory Note: This is the actual contract you sign to borrow money. This contract will identify the borrower, the lender, the amount of the loan, the *interest rate*, the repayment term (e.g., 5, 15, 30 years), etc.

Mortgage: This is a document that provides security for the lender in case you don't repay your loan. It basically says that if you don't repay, the lender can repossess your house and sell it to get its money back.

As a caveat, although the above descriptions are generally accurate, each state's laws are different and my descriptions should not be taken as a legal advice. When you are purchasing a home, your real estate agent should be able to walk you through all the nuances specific to wherever you live.

How a Home Loan Is Calculated

In this section I'll explain the most common types of home loans and show you how they are calculated. Please note Excel is needed to perform the following calculations.

Amortizing Loan

The most common type of home loan is an *amortizing loan*. All this means is that you make fixed monthly payments for a period of time until your loan is paid off. Each payment includes a portion to pay down the *principal* and a portion for *interest*. You'll often hear these referred to as fixed-rate loans, most commonly for 15 or 30 years.

Adjustable Rate Mortgage

This is a combination of a fixed-rate and a variable-rate loan. Similar to an amortizing loan, all payments include a portion for principal and a portion for interest. During the fixed period your rate does not change and is usually lower than that for a traditional amortizing loan. Once the fixed period is over, the rate will reset, typically higher, to a pre-determined benchmark (e.g., the *prime rate*) plus an additional premium. When the rate resets it becomes floating and will adjust periodically for the remainder of the term. This type of loan is usually much cheaper than an amortizing loan during the initial fixed-rate period, but more expensive than an amortizing loan in the long run. To give an example of when someone might use this type of loan, I used to work for a company that relocated its employees every 2–3 years. As employees knew they would only be in their house for a few years, most got a 5-year *adjustable rate mortgage* and were out of the house well before the rate reset.

Interest-Only Loan

For an *interest-only loan* the borrower pays only interest on the loan, with the full principal balance due at the end of the term. The payments are much cheaper than those for an amortizing loan as they do not include any portion for principal. This type of loan is popular, for example, with house flippers, as they intend to own the house for only a short period of time and want to minimize the amount tied up in the flip. The lower payments help them accomplish this, and the house flippers make their money through the increase in home value when they sell.

Calculating Your Loan Payment

There are three key components of any loan:

1. Loan Amount: This is, just as the name suggests, how much you borrow from the bank
2. *Periodic Interest Rate*: This is the interest rate that is used for your periodic payments
3. Number of Periods: The number of monthly payments you will make over the life of the loan

Let's walk through an example of how to calculate each of these components using the following assumptions.

Assumptions:
 Home Purchase Price: $400,000
 Down Payment: 20%
 Interest Rate: 3%
 Term: 30 years

Calculations:
 Loan Amount = Purchase Price − Down Payment = $400,000 − ($400,000 * 20%) = $320,000
 Periodic Interest Rate = (APR /12) = 3%/12 = 0.25%, or 0.0025 in decimal form
  If you're wondering why we divide the APR by 12, it is because the *period* (interval at which interest is charged) for a home loan is monthly (refer to Chapter 2, "Compound Interest," if you need a review).
 Number of Periods = Loan Term in Years * 12 = 30 * 12 = 360

Now that we have our inputs, we can calculate how much the monthly payments will be. Let's start with an amortizing loan as it is the most common type. As I mentioned before, you will need Excel to perform the calculations. For this example, we will use the Excel PMT (payment) function. The PMT function in Excel takes the following inputs:

Inputs:
 Rate (Periodic Interest Rate): 0.0025
 Nper (Number of Periods): 360
 PV (Loan Amount): $320,000
 FV (Future Value): 0 (this denotes the value of your loan at the end of the term and should always be 0 as your loan will be paid off)
 Type: 0 (this means you pay your loan at the end of the month)

Based on the above assumptions, your monthly fixed payment of principal and interest will be $1,349 for the next 30 years. The above function is not intuitive for most people, and I find looking at the detailed calculations a bit more helpful. Let's take a look at how the loan is actually paid down month after month.

At the end of the first month (period 1), your interest will be calculated based on the outstanding loan amount (as you have made no payments yet, the outstanding amount is still $320,000) using the periodic interest rate (interest rate divided by the number of periods in one year) of 0.25%. The calculations are as follows:

Formula:
 Interest Payment = Principal * Periodic Interest Rate
 Principal Payment = Monthly Payment − Interest Payment

Calculation:
     Interest Payment = $320,000 * 0.0025 = $800
     Principal Payment = $1,349 − $800 = $549

Your initial interest payment is $800. Your total loan payment, as calculated above, is $1,349, and the amount left over after paying interest is $549 ($1,349 − $800). This amount is applied to pay down the principal balance. As you have now paid down $549 of principal, your next interest payment will be slightly lower and more of your overall payment will go to pay down the outstanding principal. Let's continue with the example and see how your interest and principal change in month 2 (period 2).

Calculation:
     Interest Payment = $319,451 * 0.0025 = $798
     Principal Payment = $1,349 − $798 = $551

Your interest payment in month 2 is slightly lower ($798 vs. $800). The difference of $2, although small, will grow every month as your outstanding principal gets smaller. In Exhibit 8.1, you can see that by period 358 all but $10 of your monthly payment is going to principal and at the end of period 360 (end of 30 years) the principal balance is fully paid off.

Exhibit 8.1 Amortizing Loan Payoff Summary

	Period 1	Period 2	Period 3		Period 358	Period 359	Period 360
Beginning Period Balance	$320,000	$319,451	$318,900		$4,027	$2,688	$1,346
Interest Payment	($800)	($798)	($797)		($10)	($7)	($3)
Principal Payment	($549)	($551)	($552)	......	($1,339)	($1,342)	($1,346)
Total Payment	($1,349)	($1,349)	($1,349)		($1,349)	($1,349)	($1,349)
Ending Period Balance	$319,451	$318,900	$318,348		$2,688	$1,346	($0)

See the "Amortizing Loan" tab in the accompanying Excel for detailed calculations.

Next, let's take a look at an adjustable rate mortgage. In this example we will use the same assumptions as before: home purchase price of $400,000, 20% down payment, 3% interest rate, and 30-year loan. However, we will also assume the loan is a 5-year adjustable rate mortgage (i.e., the rate will reset after 5 years). The initial monthly payment calculation is the exact same as the amortizing loan example, so I won't repeat the math. The first 5 years (60 periods) of payments will be $1,349 per month.

When the loan resets, the bank will calculate a new amortizing loan using the outstanding principal at that time, the number of periods left on the loan, and the new interest rate. Let's look at an example of what happens after 5 years (60 periods) when the loan resets to a 5% interest rate.

The first step is to determine what the outstanding principal is (i.e., how much you still owe on the loan). To do this, we use the PV (*present value*) function in Excel. The PV function in Excel takes the following inputs:

Inputs:
Rate (Periodic Interest Rate): 0.0025 (this is your initial periodic rate, 3%/12)
Nper (Number of Periods): 300 (the number of periods left [360 – 60] until the loan is paid off)
PMT (Monthly Payment): –$1,394 (your monthly payment for the first 5 years)
FV (Future Value): 0 (this denotes the value of your loan at the end of the term and should always be 0 as your loan will be paid off)
Type: 0 (this means you pay your loan at the end of the month)

Based on the above assumptions the principal outstanding (i.e., PV of the loan after 5 years [60 periods]) is $284,500. Now that we know the new loan amount, we use the PMT function again to calculate the new monthly payment. The inputs are as follows:

Inputs:
Rate (Periodic Interest Rate): 0.0042 (this is your new APR of 5% divided by 12)
Nper (Number of Periods): 300 (the number of periods left until the loan is paid off)
PV (Loan Amount): $284,500
FV (Future Value): 0 (this denotes the value of your loan at the end of the term and should always be 0 as your loan will be paid off)
Type: 0 (this means you pay your loan at the end of the month)

The new payment is $1,663 per month. Because the loan reset to a 5% interest rate the payments went up by $314 per month. You would need to do the above calculations every time the loan resets to determine your new payment amount. See the "Adjustable Rate Mortgage" tab in the accompanying Excel for detailed calculations.

Lastly, let's look at an interest-only loan. The calculation for this loan is quite simple and can be done with a normal calculator. Because an interest-only loan does not amortize (i.e., the principal is not paid down), the calculation is simply the periodic interest rate multiplied by the outstanding balance. We will use the same assumptions as in the amortizing loan example: home purchase price of $400,000, 20% down payment, 3% interest rate, and 30-year loan. The formula and calculations are as follows:

Formula:
Interest Payment = Principal * Periodic Interest Rate
$320,000 * 0.0025 = $800

Your monthly payment is $800 and that all goes to interest. The benefit of this type of loan is a much smaller payment; however, your principal balance is never paid down. You will pay $800 per month until period 360 (i.e., the last payment of the loan) when you pay the last interest payment and the full principal of $320,000 back. See the "Interest-only loan" tab in the accompanying Excel for detailed calculations.

Costs of Home Ownership

As I mentioned at the beginning of the chapter, the cost of owning a home is not limited to your promissory note (i.e., your monthly loan payment); there is also property tax, insurance, maintenance, Homeowners Association fees, and side projects. Let's go through an example of the costs you will likely encounter when owning a home.

Promissory Note Payment

Let's assume you intend to purchase a home for $400,000. We will also assume a 20% down payment, a 3% interest rate, and a 30-year loan (these are the same assumptions used in the previous amortizing loan example). To calculate the payment, use the Excel PMT (payment) function. The inputs are as follows:

Inputs:
> Rate (Periodic Interest Rate): 0.0025
> Nper (Number of Periods): 360
> PV (Loan Amount): $320,000
> FV (Future Value): 0 (this denotes the value of your loan at the end of the term and should always be 0 as your loan will be paid off)
> Type: 0 (this means you pay your loan at the end of the month)

Based on the above assumptions, your monthly fixed payment of principal and interest will be $1,349 per month for the next 30 years.

Property Taxes

Property taxes can vary greatly depending on where you live. In addition to this variability, you can also protest your home appraisal value to most taxing authorities. You can do this yourself by submitting the necessary paperwork to your local taxing authority or hire a tax consulting firm such as O'Connor & Associates[11] to protest on your behalf. While I do not endorse any particular firm, I have personally used O'Connor & Associates and have been satisfied with their service and results.

In addition, in some jurisdictions (such as the United States) if the house is your primary residence, by submitting a Homestead Exemption form you can get a slight reduction in the property tax rate. The purpose of this section is not to go into depth about how to reduce your property tax rates, but just to let you know those options are available.

Property taxes are paid to the local government every year and calculated based on the appraised value of your home. In this example, we will assume the property tax rate is 2.5% and the appraisal value is the same as the purchase price of $400,000.

The formula and calculation is as follows:

Formula:

House Value * Property Tax Rate

Calculation:

$400,000 * 0.025 = $10,000

Your yearly taxes due will be $10,000, or $833 monthly.

Insurance

Property insurance will also differ greatly depending on where you live. For example, if you live in a flood zone or somewhere prone to earthquakes, your costs will likely be much higher. Also, banks typically require you to maintain insurance on the house until it is paid off. So if you live in an area with expensive insurance there is no getting out of it. For this example we'll assume $100 per month.

As a side note, although I have used a 20% down payment for this example, if your down payment is less than 20%, lenders will also require you to purchase private mortgage insurance. This insurance protects the lender from losses in case, for whatever reason, you default on your loan. This insurance is required only if you put less than 20% down, so as soon as you have paid down at least 20% of the principal you can cancel this insurance and eliminate the extra expense.[12]

Maintenance

This cost is unavoidable and is a combination of planned and unplanned maintenance. Examples of planned maintenance are weekly and seasonal yard maintenance, yearly AC servicing, and interior/exterior painting. Examples of unplanned maintenance are garbage disposal replacement, plumbing leaks, roof issues, broken sprinklers – the list goes on. While the exact timing of these costs may not be fully known, you can be 100% certain you will incur them. This is why it's prudent to save for them so you are not caught off-guard with no way to pay. Assume $200 per month for maintenance costs.

Homeowners Association Fees

Nowadays most single-family homes, townhomes, and condos have monthly Homeowners Association (HOA) fees. These HOA fees are in addition to your monthly loan payment, taxes, etc. and are charged in perpetuity (i.e., forever).

For neighborhoods with single-family homes, the traditional role of an HOA was to act as an independent third party to ensure residents upheld basic standards. Each home would pay a small monthly fee and the HOA would take action for any violations of neighborhood rules (e.g., your neighbors let their front yard turn into a jungle or decide to paint their house pink). As neighborhood amenities have grown over the years (many communities now come with swimming pools, tennis courts, etc. as standard), so have the role and fees of HOAs. Particularly for townhomes and condos, as they usually have many shared amenities, the HOA functions more as a facilities management company and subsequently charges higher fees. As the role and services provided by HOAs vary by community or building, before purchasing a property you should do your due diligence and ensure you are not being charged an excessive amount for the services received.

Let's take a closer look at the added cost of HOA fees over the lifetime of home ownership and continue with the above example. We assume the following: the home purchase price is $400,000, HOA fees are $300 per month, and a low-risk deposit at your local bank pays 2.5%. We can determine the present value of the HOA fees by calculating how much you need to invest to generate $300 per month. Because the HOA fees are paid in perpetuity (i.e., forever), we will use a perpetuity formula to calculate the present value of the investment needed. For this no Excel is needed and the math can be done using a basic calculator. The formula and calculation are as follows:

Formula:
   Yearly Investment Income Needed/Interest Rate

Inputs:
   Yearly Investment Income Needed: $3,600 ($300 per month * 12)
   Interest Rate: 2.5% (rate of return your bank will pay for funds you invest)

Calculation:
   $3,600/0.025 = $144,000

To generate enough investment return to pay the HOA fees you have to deposit $144,000 ($144,000 * 2.5% = $3,600) at your local bank. This is the same as increasing the purchase price of the house by $144,000. So although a $300 per month HOA fee may sound reasonable, it's actually quite expensive.

In summary, HOA fees aren't inherently bad, but you should be very skeptical and pay close attention to what you are getting in return. As shown by this example, a seemingly small monthly fee can add significant cost to home ownership.

Side Projects

Everyone wants to put a personal touch on a home, and this inevitably results in side projects. Trust me, you will become very familiar with your local hardware shop! Some examples are installing new window shades, adding new knobs to the kitchen cabinets, painting an accent wall, and installing new light fixtures. These costs will be different for everyone, but the one thing that's certain is that you will spend money on side projects. Assume $200 per month for side projects.

I have summarized the full estimated monthly cost of home ownership in Exhibit 8.2.

Exhibit 8.2 Estimated Monthly Cost of Home Ownership

Monthly Payment	($1,349)
Property Tax	($833)
Insurance	($100)
Maintenance	($200)
HOA Fees	($300)
Side Projects	($200)
Total	($2,982)

In this example, the monthly payment is only $1,349, but the real monthly cost you are likely to incur is $2,982, which is more than double.

How Much Can You Afford?

A good sanity check to do when determining whether you can afford a home is to see how much you need to earn to meet the monthly cost. To do this the formula and calculations are as follows:

Formula:

Monthly Cost of Home Ownership/(1 − Tax Rate)

We divide the total cost by (1 − Tax Rate) because your take-home earnings are after tax. So you actually need to make more than $2,982 because you will have to pay taxes out of your earnings as well. If we assume your tax rate is 15%, the calculation is as follows:

Calculation:

$2,982/(1 − 0.15) = $2,982/0.85 = $3,509

You need to make $3,509 per month (pre-tax) to have enough after-tax dollars left over to pay for your house. On a yearly basis you will need $42,105:

($2,982 * 12)/(1 − 0.15) = $35,790/0.85 = $42,105

Please note, these are just estimates and your actual cost for any of these items may be higher or lower. Also, keep in mind this is just for the house itself. You will actually need to make considerably more than $42,105 as you still need to account for any other necessary expenses you have such as car or student loan payments, utilities, food, and transportation.

You will also be limited by how much the lender (i.e., the bank) is willing to let you borrow. According to Investopedia,[13] a good rule of thumb is that no more than 28% of your gross income (i.e., pre-tax income) should go to your promissory note repayment, property tax, and insurance. This is also known as the *front-end ratio*. While each lender's requirements will be different, as your front-end ratio increases, lenders will either offer you a lower loan amount or increase your interest rate or both. To get the best line of sight on how much you can borrow, a good idea is to apply for pre-approval with potential lenders. When you apply to get pre-approved, the lender will run a credit check, you will submit various information such as employment history, tax returns, other sources of income, and monthly expenses, and then the lender will officially tell you how much they are willing to let you borrow and at what interest rate. This not only helps to guide your budget when shopping for a house, but is also very helpful when bidding on a house as potential sellers know you are serious about making an offer and have access to funds to complete the purchase.[14] One other thing to keep in mind is that you do not have to borrow the full amount you are pre-approved for. Ultimately, you are accountable for repaying the funds and it is your responsibility to act as a final check to ensure you do not take on too much debt.

Lastly, the important takeaway is to make sure you account for the full costs and understand how it will impact your overall budget when making your purchase decision.

See the "Cost of Home Ownership" tab in the accompanying Excel for detailed calculations

15 or 30 Year Loan?

There are two things to consider when choosing between a 15-year and a 30-year amortizing loan. The first is which you can afford. The payments on a 15-year loan will always be more because you are paying pack the principal over a shorter period of time. For the majority of people purchasing their primary home, affordability is the determining factor. The other factor to consider is *opportunity cost*. While also applicable to purchasing a primary home, opportunity cost becomes more relevant when purchasing a home as an investment property. If you can afford both the 15 and the 30-year loans, you should evaluate your options for what else you could do with the extra money you have to pay for the 15-year vs. the 30-year note. Let's take a more in-depth look at the first criterion, affordability, and compare some of the trade-offs of the 15 vs. 30-year loan.

Affordability

A 15-year note will always have a higher monthly payment. This is because you are paying back the loan over a shorter time (180 vs. 360 periods). However, because the loan term is shorter, a 15-year note will always have a lower interest rate. Remember from Chapter 1 ("Time Value of Money") that interest has two components: *inflation* and *risk*. Because the lender (i.e., the bank) gets paid back 15 years earlier, they incur less risk. Also, because the loan is shorter, by 15 years, there is less inflation. So the increase in monthly payment will always be partly offset by a lower interest rate. Let's take a look at an example and compare monthly payments for a 15-year and a 30-year loan. We will use the same assumptions as in the previous examples for the 30-year amortizing loan (home purchase price of $400,000, a 20% down payment, and a 3% interest rate); for the 15-year amortizing loan the differences will be a lower interest rate of 2.5% and a 15-year (i.e., 180 periods) term. For the 30-year loan, we know from the previous calculations the monthly payment is $1,349. For the 15-year loan, again we use the Excel PMT (payment) function. The inputs are as follows:

Inputs:
    Rate (Periodic Interest Rate): 0.21% (0.0021 in decimal form)
    Nper (Number of Periods): 180
    PV (Loan Amount): $320,000
    FV (Future Value): 0 (this denotes the value of your loan at the end of the term and should always
        be 0 as your loan will be paid off)
    Type: 0 (this means you pay your loan at the end of the month)

Based on the above assumptions your monthly fixed payment of principal and interest will be $2,134 for the next 15 years. This is $785 per month more than for the 30-year loan. While the monthly payments are more expensive, you save money on interest in the long run. The amount of interest paid over 30 years is $165,688 vs. $64,071 over 15 years. So by making higher payments over a shorter period of time you save $101,617 of interest.

To calculate the total interest paid for the two loans, we use the Excel CUMIPMT (cumulative interest) function. (See the "15 vs. 30 Year Loan" tab in the accompanying spreadsheet for detailed calculations.) The CUMIPMT function in Excel takes the following inputs:

30-Year Loan

Inputs:
    Rate (Periodic Interest Rate): 0.25% (0.0025 in decimal form)
    Nper (Number of Periods): 360
    PV (Loan Amount): $320,000
    Start Period: 1 (this just says you want to sum the interest from the 1st month)
    End Period: 360 (this tells the function how many periods until your loan will be paid off)
    Type: 0 (this means you pay your loan at the end of the month)

15-Year Loan

Inputs:
    Rate (Periodic Interest Rate): 0.21% (0.0021 in decimal form)
    Nper (Number of Periods): 180
    PV (Loan Amount): $320,000
    Start Period: 1 (this just says you want to sum the interest from the 1st month)
    End Period: 180 (this tells the function how many periods until your loan will be paid off)
    Type: 0 (this means you pay your loan at the end of the month)

While affordability may ultimately dictate whether you choose the 15 or 30-year loan, the important thing to remember is the trade-off for the lower monthly payments of the 30-year loan is more interest paid over the life of the loan.

Opportunity Cost

As I mentioned previously, this section is more applicable to purchasing a home as an investment. The important assumption here is that regardless of which loan you go with, you will pay or invest the amount of the 15 year loan ($2,134) every month over the next 30 years. Continuing with the above example, assume you can spend $2,134 per month (i.e., enough to cover either the 15 or the 30-year loan payment). If you go for the 30-year loan you will have $785 ($2,134 – 1,349) left over and will invest that amount every month for the next 30 years. If you go with the 15-year loan you will make repayments of $2,134 for the first 15 years and for the last 15 years you will invest that amount every month. To compare the two options we can look at their respective future value (i.e., value after 30 years). Let's assume you can get a 5% *annual percentage rate* as your return for both investments and look at the 30-year option first. We will use the Excel FV (future value) function. (See the "Opportunity Cost of 15 Yr Loan" tab in the accompanying Excel for details.) The FV function in Excel takes the following inputs:

Inputs:

    Rate (Periodic Interest Rate): 0.42% (0.0042 in decimal form; this is the APR of 5%/12)

    Nper (Number of Periods): 360 (this represents 30 years)

    PMT (Payment): $785 (this is the amount left over after the monthly payment for the 30-year loan, i.e., $2,134 – $1,349)

    PV (Loan Amount): 0 (this is because on day 1 you have nothing invested; you will make your first investment at the end of the first month)

    Type: 0 (this means you will invest the money at the end of every month)

At the end of 30 years, your investment will have grown to $652,984.

Now let's look at the future value if you go with the 15-year option and invest $2,134 every month after the house is paid off (i.e., starting after 15 years, from period 181). Again will use the Excel FV (future value) function. The inputs are as follows:

Inputs:

    Rate (Periodic Interest Rate): 0.42% (0.0042 in decimal form; this is the APR of 5%/12)

    Nper (Number of Periods): 180 (this represents the last 15 years of the 30 years)

    PMT (Payment): $2,134 (the full amount is available to invest after the loan is paid off)

    PV (Loan Amount): 0 (this is because on day 1 you have nothing invested)

    Type: 0 (this means you will invest the money at the end of every month)

At the end of 30 years, if you choose the 15-year loan option and invest the loan amount during the last 15 years (i.e., once the house is paid off) you will end up with only $570,321. So it is actually better to take a 30-year loan at a higher interest rate, because by investing the difference you will end up with more money at the end of 30 years.

To understand the minimum investment return needed to make the 30-year loan a better option, see the sensitivity analysis in Exhibit 8.3. As long as the investment return is above approximately 3.5%, the 30-year loan is the better option.

Exhibit 8.3 Opportunity Cost of 15 vs. 30 Year Loan Sensitivity Analysis

Rate of Return on Investment	Future Value of Investment with 15-Year Loan	Future Value of Investment with 30-Year Loan
3.0%	484,297	457,211
3.5%	504,170	498,540
4.0%	525,090	544,546
4.5%	547,119	595,809
5.0%	570,321	652,984
5.5%	594,766	716,813
6.0%	620,527	788,135

Also, the difference in interest rates of the 15 and 30-year loans will influence which loan is more attractive. As the 30-year loan interest rate becomes more expensive relative to the 15-year rate (i.e., as the difference between the two loan rates increases), the greater the investment return will need to be before the 30-year loan generates a higher future value.

Let's continue with the above example, but now assume the rate on the 15-year loan has dropped to 1.5% and the 30-year rate remains at 3%. While the monthly payments for the 30-year loan will remain unchanged at $1,349, the payments for the 15-year loan will decrease to $1,986. The difference is now only $637 per month, whereas in the previous example the difference was $785 per month. Because the difference is lower, the amount you will invest every month is also lower, and the future value will not be as much in 30 years. Assuming a 5% return, we can run another sensitivity analysis using different assumed interest rates to see how low the 15-year rate needs to be to give it a higher future value than the 30-year option.

The sensitivity analysis in Exhibit 8.4 shows that the interest rate for the 15-year loan must be 1.5% or lower for the future value of the investment to be more than for the 30-year loan.

**Exhibit 8.4 Opportunity Cost of 15 vs. 30-Year Loan
Sensitivity Analysis, Assuming a 5% Return**

Rate for 30-Year Loan	Rate for 15-Year Loan	Interest Rate Difference	Future Value of Investment with 15-Year Loan	Future Value of Investment with 30-Year Loan
3.0%	0.5%	2.5%	493,321	413,229
3.0%	1.0%	2.0%	511,907	471,100
3.0%	1.5%	1.5%	530,937	530,352
3.0%	2.0%	1.0%	550,409	590,983
3.0%	2.5%	0.5%	570,321	652,984
3.0%	3.0%	0.0%	590,671	716,349

Although the above example seems clear cut, there are several other things to consider. We assume a return of 5% per year, every year, for 30 years. This assumption, while necessary to complete the calculations, is completely unrealistic. In reality the returns will vary year to year (i.e., the 5% is not 100% guaranteed). Even if the arithmetic average of returns is 5%, the order of returns will also fluctuate (i.e., some years will be higher than 5% and some lower). The order of these returns will greatly impact the amount you end up with after 30 years. By investing you have the potential to generate a higher return, but you also bear higher risk. Conversely, what is 100% guaranteed is that your bank will expect the payments to be made every month. So, even though taking the 30-year loan and investing the difference seems like a better option, you should perform a sensitivity analysis for the rate of return and risk adjust the return because it is not 100% guaranteed (i.e., lower the expected investment returns depending on your degree of confidence).

Should You Pay Off Your House Early?

Let's say you took out a 30-year loan. A few years have gone by and you now have extra money to either make additional monthly payments or pay the house off in full. From a purely financial perspective, if you can invest the extra money to generate a higher return than the interest rate you are paying on your loan, you should not pay off the house early. However, as I mentioned before, there is 100% certainty that your bank will require you to make the monthly payments, but your investment returns are not 100% guaranteed. Therefore you need to consider how confident you are that you can in fact achieve your estimated investment returns. If you are not 100% certain, you should adjust the estimated return downward to match your degree of confidence. The other thing to consider is what I like to call the "sleep at night factor." In particular for your primary residence, the peace of mind that comes with having your home bought and paid for is difficult to quantify, and the potential to generate an extra percent or two of return may not be worth the risk.

Lastly, when making any extra payments to your loan, it is extremely important to make sure the amount is applied to the principal. Typically, it's as simple as checking a box on the bank's website, and some banks will even automatically apply any additional amount to principal. However, each bank's policies are unique, and you need to clarify the process to make sure any additional amount you pay goes to the principal.

Refinancing

Another decision you will likely have to make is whether or not to refinance. *Refinancing* involves taking out a new loan at a lower interest rate to pay off an existing loan with a higher interest rate. Because taking out any loan involves fees, the savings from the lower interest rate are partly eroded by those fees. The fees are typically added to the principal amount of the new loan amount. The two criteria to evaluate whether refinancing makes sense are as follows:

1. Breakeven: Assuming you continue to make the same payments as before you refinanced (i.e., you will now be paying extra toward principal every month), how long will it take you to pay down the added principal from fees?
2. Overall Savings: How much less will you spend in total after refinancing than you would have spent if you'd kept the original loan?

In this example we assume you can still afford to make your existing payments and after you refinance you will continue to make the same payments as before. This will of course shorten the time until your loan is repaid; however, it will take time to offset the bank fees for the new loan. Let's make the following assumptions for the initial loan: a home value of $400,000, an interest rate of 5%, and a 30-year loan. Monthly payments will be $1,718. After 5 years (60 periods) rates have dropped significantly and you can get a new 30-year loan at 2%. The outstanding balance on the existing loan after 5 years is $293,816 (refer to the adjustable rate mortgage calculations in the "Calculating Your Loan Payment" section for how to calculate the present value of an outstanding loan). In addition, the bank will charge you fees of 3% of the outstanding balance of your existing loan ($293,816 * 3% = $8,816) and add that to the new loan amount. So, to refinance your existing loan of $293,816, you will borrow $302,668 ($293,816 + $8,816). For the new loan, we assume the amount borrowed is $302,668, the interest rate is 2%, and the term 30 years. The new monthly payments will be $1,119, or $599 ($1,718 − $1,119) per month cheaper than your previous loan. Based on these new assumptions there are two data points we need to look at: the number of periods until breakeven and the overall savings.

Breakeven

This shows how many periods it will take to recoup the refinancing cost. We can calculate this by comparing the outstanding balance for each period of the new loan with what the outstanding balance of the original loan would have been. As you can see from Exhibit 8.5, in period 13 the outstanding balance becomes less for the new loan. In other words it takes 13 months to recoup the financing costs. This is fairly quick because the new loan payments are reduced by $599 per month.

See the "Refinance after 5 Yrs" tab in the accompanying Excel for detailed calculations.

Exhibit 8.5 Refinancing Breakeven Calculation Summary

	Period 1	Period 2	Period 3		Period 11	Period 12	Period 13
Beginning Period Balance	$302,668	$301,454	$300,239		$290,442	$289,208	$287,973
Interest Payment	($504)	($502)	($500)		($484)	($482)	($480)
Principal Payment	($614)	($616)	($618)		($635)	($637)	($639)
Additional Payment	($599)	($599)	($599)	......	($599)	($599)	($599)
Total Payment	($1,718)	($1,718)	($1,718)		($1,718)	($1,718)	($1,718)
Ending Period Balance of New Loan	**$301,454**	**$300,239**	**$299,021**		**$289,208**	**$287,973**	**$286,735**
End of Period Balance of Original Loan	$293,358	$292,863	$292,365		$288,310	$287,793	$287,274
Difference	($8,096)	($7,376)	($6,656)		($899)	($180)	$539

If you continue to make the same monthly payment of $1,718, the additional $599 will go to pay down principal rather than going to interest and the loan will be paid off after 209 periods (Exhibit 8.6).

Exhibit 8.6 Refinancing Payoff Calculation Summary

	Period 1	Period 2	Period 3		Period 207	Period 208	Period 209
Beginning Period Balance	$302,668	$301,454	$300,239		$4,732	$3,022	$1,309
Interest Payment	($504)	($502)	($500)		($8)	($5)	($2)
Principal Payment	($614)	($616)	($618)		($1,111)	($1,114)	($1,117)
Additional Payment	($599)	($599)	($599)	......	($599)	($599)	($192)
Total Payment	($1,718)	($1,718)	($1,718)		($1,718)	($1,718)	($1,311)
Ending Period Balance of New Loan	**$301,454**	**$300,239**	**$299,021**		**$3,022**	**$1,309**	**$0**

See the "Refinance after 5 Yrs" tab in the accompanying Excel for detailed calculations.

Overall Savings

To calculate the overall savings, we simply compare the total amount you have left to pay for the original 30-year loan with the total amount you will pay for the new loan. First, we calculate the remaining amount for the original loan. This is simply your original payment of $1,718 times 300 (i.e., the number of payments left), which is $515,349 (the monthly payment of $1,718 is rounded to the nearest dollar; for the exact calculation please refer to the Excel file). Assuming you continue to make the same monthly payment as before, the amount you will have to pay for the new loan is calculated as follows:

Calculations:

> New Loan = $358,620
>
> (This represents the exact amount. The monthly payment of $1,718 used below is rounded to the nearest dollar. For the exact calculation please refer to the Excel file.)
>
> a. Periods 1–208 (~$1,718 * 208) = $357,309
>
> b. Period 209 = $ 1,311
>
> > Because additional principal payments have been made, in period 209 only $1,311 (not the full payment of $1,718) is required.

The total you pay after refinancing is $358,620. Not only do you pay the house off sooner by 91 months (360 – 269 periods), but you save $156,729 ($515,349 – $358,620) compared with what you would have paid if you'd stuck with the original loan.

This is all summarized in Exhibit 8.7. See the "Refinance after 5 Yrs" tab in the accompanying Excel for detailed calculations.

Exhibit 8.7 Refinancing Overall Savings Summary

Periods to Breakeven	**13**
Periods Until Refinance Loan Is Paid Off	**209**
Total Payments from Original Loan	($618,419)
Total Payments If You Refinance (includes original loan payments before refinancing + refinancing payments)	($461,689)
Total Savings	**$156,729**

This has been by far the most complicated chapter of the book, not only because of all the calculations involved, but also because of the multitude of variables. I recommend you familiarize yourself with the "Refinance after 5 Yrs" tab of the accompanying Excel. If you input your specific data into the yellow-highlighted cells, the file will perform the calculations for you and make it easy to test many different scenarios. This will allow you to focus less on the detailed calculations and more on understanding the key outputs you need to evaluate the decision to refinance.

9

KIDS

I went back and forth about whether to write this chapter and realize I will probably catch a bit of heat for what I am going to say. But I think it's something that needs to be talked about as it is not discussed enough.

First, let me say that I love my family. I am happily married, have two beautiful children, and would not trade my family for anything. However, raising kids is HARD! In the base case, kids put a ton of stress on a marriage, and adding financial strain on top of that can often push things over the top. Kids are wonderful and bring you joy in all kinds of ways, and I am in no way advocating not having children. However, what I am saying is that you should make sure you are prepared financially for the burden of children so you can focus on loving them instead of stressing about your finances. At this point you are probably thinking, "Yeah, I know kids are expensive – everyone knows that." But do you really know the financial impact of having kids?

Let's quantify and look at some hard numbers.

In this chapter, we will do the following:

1. Identify potential *opportunity costs* associated with kids
2. Identify financial obligations that come with kids
3. Quantify the opportunity costs and financial obligations of having kids

Opportunity Costs

The main opportunity cost associated with children is that they limit your earnings potential. This happens in two ways:

Job Advancement: Once kids come into the picture, many people are not willing to work the long hours required to move higher up in a company. As I mentioned before, making it to executive comes with many financial benefits but also requires many long days and nights in the office. This comes at the price of sacrificing time with the family, and many parents are not willing to make the trade-off. Mobility is also an issue: parents are more reluctant to move for better job opportunities as they don't want to uproot their children. You should consider these trade-offs (lower future salary for more time with your family; lack of mobility for greater stability for your children) before you have kids.

Lost Spousal Income: Many parents with young children choose either to stay at home or to reduce their work hours. This is an explicit cost as you miss out on the future earnings you otherwise would have made.

Financial Obligations

In addition to lower potential future earnings, kids come with other costs. Each family will have their own idea of what they are willing to spend and what costs they deem reasonable, but at a minimum you can expect the typical expenses for food, clothes, field trips, tuition, extracurricular activities – and the list goes on.

Quantify the Costs

Let's continue with the plumber example from Chapter 5 ("Choosing the Right Career"). Assume you and your spouse are plumbers, both 28 years old, and are getting ready to have your first child. You and your spouse are currently working and own a home that is big enough for a family of four. Your spouse has decided to work half time (20 hours per week) once the baby is born and will continue to work half time until retirement. We will also assume you will have only one child. To calculate the costs, we need to quantify the opportunity cost of your spouse working half time and the cost of the additional expenses associated with the child.

Let's tackle the opportunity cost first and use the following assumptions:

Assumptions:

Work Years: 30 *periods* (will start working half time on 28th birthday, assume January 1, and will retire at the end of the year age 57)

Inflation: 3% (the amount we will discount future earnings by to get them in today's dollars)

Wage Inflation: 2%

Wage: $54,221 (this is what your spouse will be earning after 10 years if the starting wage was $44,480)

To get the future salary of $54,221 use the *compound interest* formula (refer back to the "Calculating the Future Value" section in Chapter 4 if you need a review). The formula, inputs, and calculations are as follows:

Formula:

$$Principal * (1 + Interest\ Rate)^{Number\ of\ Periods}$$

Inputs:

> Principal: $44,480 (starting salary)
> Interest Rate: 2% (wage inflation rate)
> Periods: 10 (how many years your spouse has been working)

Calculation:

> $44,480 * (1 + 0.02)^{10} = $44,480 * 1.219 = $54,221

Effective Tax Rate: 15% (estimated average tax rate paid on all earnings. The effective tax rate for the starting salary is around 15% and as both the salary and tax brackets will grow in line with inflation, we use this rate for the entire time frame)

To determine the opportunity cost, we first need to use the above assumptions and calculate the after-tax *present value* (i.e., value of future earnings in today's dollars) of the estimated net earnings (i.e., earnings – debt payments) from age 28 to age 57 (i.e., 30 calculations) if your spouse had not had the child and had worked full time. Let's look at years 1 and 2; to see all 30 calculations please refer to the "Opportunity Cost of Kids" tab in the accompanying Excel.

Year 1 (Age 28)

Inputs:

> Earnings: $54,221 (the wage at age 28 from the assumptions above)
> Taxes: −$8,133 (tax rate of 15% applied to earnings of $54,221 [$54,221 * 15%]; this is negative because taxes are subtracted from earnings)
> Student Debt Repayment: $0 (because the plumber has no debt)
> *Discount Rate*: $1.03^1 = (1 + \text{Inflation Rate})^{\text{Number of Periods}}$
> This is the factor by which we reduce future earnings. The number of periods represents how many years you are away from today, and as the number of periods grows so will the discount rate.

Calculation:

> Net Earnings: $54,221 − $8,133 = $46,088
> Present Value of After-Tax Earnings: $46,088/1.03 = $44,745

Year 2 (Age 29)

Inputs:

> Earnings: $55,305 (wage from year 1 inflated by 2% [$54,221 * 1.02])
> Taxes: −$8,296 (tax rate of 15% applied to earnings of $55,305 [$55,305 * 15%]; this is negative because taxes are subtracted from earnings)
> Student Debt Repayment: $0 (because the plumber has no debt)
> Discount Rate: $1.0609 = 1.03^2 = (1 + \text{Inflation Rate})^{\text{Number of Periods}}$

Calculation:

> Net Earnings: $55,305 − $8,296 = $47,009
> Present Value of After-Tax Earnings: $47,009/1.0609 = $44,311

Perform the same calculations as above for each subsequent period (i.e., age 30–57), and then sum the after-tax present value of each year's earnings to get a present value of earnings for the plumber for working full time from age 28 to age 57 of $1,169,444. These calculations are summarized in Exhibit 9.1.

Exhibit 9.1 Present Value of Plumber Lifetime Earnings Summary

Assumptions			Year 1	Year 2	Year 3		Year 28	Year 29	Year 30
Education Loan	$0	Age at Beginning of Year	28	29	30		55	56	57
Work Years	30	Full Year Earnings	$54,221	$55,305	$56,411		$92,549	$94,400	$96,228
Inflation	3.00%	Taxes	($8,133)	($8,296)	($8,462)	....	($13,133)	($14,160)	($14,433)
Wage Inflation	2.00%	Student Debt Repayment	$0	$0	$0		$0	$0	$0
Starting Wage	$54,221	Net Earnings	$46,088	$47,009	$47,950		$78,667	$80,240	$81,845
Effective tax rate	15.00%	Discount Rate							
		Formula	1.03^1	1.03^2	1.03^3		1.03^28	1.03^29	1.03^30
Present Value of Total		Discount Rate	1.0300	1.0609	1.0927		2.2879	2.3566	2.4273
Tax Earnings	1,169,444	Present Value of After Tax Earnings	$44,745	$44,311	$43,881		$34,383	$34,049	$33,719

Next we run the same calculation but assume the salary is half due to working only half time. The inputs are as follows:

Year 1 (Age 28)

Inputs:

Earnings: $27,110 (half the year 1 wage from the assumptions above)

Taxes: –$4,067 (tax rate of 15% applied to earnings of $27,110 [$27,110 * 15%]; this is negative because taxes are subtracted from earnings)

Student Debt Repayment: $0 (because the plumber has no debt)

Discount Rate: $1.03^1 = (1 + \text{Inflation Rate})^{\text{Number of Periods}}$

Calculation:

Net Earnings: $27,110 – $4,067 = $23,044

Present Value of After-Tax Earnings: $23,044/1.03 = $22,373

Notice the present value for year 1 is exactly half ($22,373 vs. $44,745) of the value in the full-time example. As the salary is cut in half, the present value of future earnings will be exactly half as well. Therefore, the present value of earnings from age 28 to age 57 is reduced to $584,722, or exactly half of the amount from working full time.

For detailed calculations see the "Opportunity Cost of Kids" tab in the accompanying Excel.

Next let's calculate the present value of the additional financial obligations. We will make the following assumptions (with all costs being annual):

Additional Costs:
  Food: $6,000
  Clothes: $500
  Extracurricular: $6,000 (includes such things as tutoring for math or reading, soccer, baseball, or any other clubs the child is involved in)
  College Savings: $6,000
  Health Insurance: $1,200
  Miscellaneous: $1,200 (toys, birthday parties, play dates, etc.)
  This totals to $20,900 per year. This is just an estimate, and each family's actual spend will be different.

Periods You Will Incur Costs: 22 (assume your child will be financially independent after 22 years and require no further support)
Cost Inflation: 4% (college and health costs typically have much higher inflation rates than the general inflation rate, and therefore the cost inflation is slightly above the overall inflation rate of 3%)
Inflation: 3% (the amount we will discount future costs by to get them in today's dollars)

We can perform the same present value calculations as above to calculate the cost. The inputs are as follows:

Year 1 (Age 28)
Inputs:
  Year 1 Additional Financial Obligation: $20,900
  Discount Rate: $1.03^1 = (1 + \text{Inflation Rate})^{\text{Number of Periods}}$

Calculation:
  Present Value of Additional Financial Obligation: $20,900/1.03 = $20,291

Year 2 (Age 29)
Inputs:
  Year 2 Additional Financial Obligation: $21,736 (this is the year 1 obligation inflated by 4% [$20,900 * 1.04])
  Discount Rate: $1.0609 = 1.03^2 = (1 + \text{Inflation Rate})^{\text{Number of Periods}}$

Calculation:
  Present Value of Additional Financial Obligation: $21,736/1.0609 = $20,488

Notice the present value of the obligation is more in year 2 than in year 1 ($20,488 vs. $20,291). This is because cost inflation was higher than general inflation (4% vs. 3%).

As with the previous examples, these calculations need to be repeated for the remaining years during which you will provide financial support to the child (i.e., years 3–22) and then summed to get the total present value of the additional financial obligation.

The total cost in today's dollars comes to $495,002. For detailed calculations see the "Kids Financial Obligation" tab in the accompanying Excel. A summary is provided in Exhibit 9.2.

Exhibit 9.2 Present Value of Additional Financial Obligations Summary

Assumptions (Yearly Cost)	
Years Until Child is Financially Independent	22
Food	$6,000
Cloths	$500
Extracurricular	$6,000
College Savings	$6,000
Health Insurance	$1,200
Misc.	$1,200
Total Additional Yearly Obligation	$20,900
Cost Inflation	4.00%
Inflation	3.00%

Present Value of Total Future Costs	$495,002

	Year 1	Year 2	Year 3		Year 20	Year 21	Year 22
Age at Beginning of Year	28	29	30		47	48	49
Total Additional Yearly Obligation	$20,900	$21,736	$22,605	.....	$44,033	$45,794	$47,626
Discount Factor Formula	1.03^1	1.03^2	1.03^3		1.03^20	1.03^21	1.03^22
Discount Factor	1.0300	1.0609	1.0927		1.8061	1.8603	1.9161
Present Value of Costs	$20,291	$20,488	$20,687		$24,380	$24,617	$24,856

If you combine this with the lost income of $584,722 calculated in the previous section, the total cost comes to $1,079,724.

As thorough as I tried to be with this example, the truth is there is no 100% accurate way to quantify how much kids cost. But I'm sure if you ask any parent, he or she will agree that kids are darn expensive.

I want to note that I didn't forget about all the intangibles that come with kids (the bonds you form, the joy of watching their faces light up from new experiences, etc.), and you should absolutely take those into account when deciding when and whether to have children. But these intangibles are different and have different value for everyone, so I purposely kept this chapter focused on what is quantifiable. In summary, you need to think through what you're getting yourself into before having kids and make sure you're financially prepared before taking the plunge.

10

LIFE INSURANCE

Most people don't think of buying life insurance as a financial decision. In fact, most people don't like to think about life insurance at all, because doing so requires you to think about your own death. Although uncomfortable, the reality is that we all die eventually and should be prepared. Life insurance has a place in all financial portfolios, not from the perspective that it will make you money, but from the perspective that it will help you keep what you have worked so very hard to get and take care of your loved ones. This chapter is not a deep dive into the plethora of insurance products available; insurance is a broad and complicated topic, and to cover it all is beyond the scope of this book. In this chapter I will focus specifically on whole life and term policies.

Whole Life vs. Term Policies

When people think of life insurance, they most often think of a whole life policy. With a whole life policy you pay premiums until you die, and upon your death a lump sum is paid to whoever you designated as the beneficiary. Because it is a 100% certainty that you will die, the insurance company will have to pay out (assuming you continue to pay your premiums). And because the payout is certain, whole life policies can be quite expensive.

A term life policy, as the name implies, is not until death but for a specific term (i.e., period of time). With a term policy you will not pay premiums after the end of the set term, and the premiums you do pay will likely be much less than those for a whole life policy. This is because there is a much lower probability the insurance company will have to pay out when the policy is for a fixed term and not until death.

As an aside, the beneficiary can be anyone you designate. Typically, beneficiaries are a spouse or child, but they can also be parents, friends, etc.

When to Purchase a Whole Life vs. a Term Policy

For most people the real need for life insurance comes not when they die of old age, but to help if they die unexpectedly while they still have significant liabilities (e.g., a large outstanding mortgage balance or small children). Let me give you an example. Let's say you are 35 years old, have an outstanding mortgage, and a spouse and two small children who rely on you for financial support. If you die unexpectedly, you will still have significant liabilities outstanding. You can purchase a term policy for 30 years to expire at age 65. At 65 years old, you anticipate you will have a decent amount of savings to get you through retirement, the house will be paid off, and your children, hopefully, will be off the payroll. In other words, your liabilities will be met and you will no longer need insurance. In addition, assuming you are currently in good health, it is statistically unlikely you will die from non-accidental causes before age 65, so the insurance company will likely not have to pay out any benefits and therefore, a term life policy can be quite affordable.

So why do people purchase whole life policies? Think of a whole life policy as a term policy with the added feature of tax-efficient estate transfer. What this means is that if you die with significant outstanding financial obligations (e.g., you need to pay your house off or pay for college for your kids), it will act like the term policy and your family can use it to meet those obligations. If you die after your financial obligations are met, a lump sum is usually paid to your designated beneficiary tax free (insurance payouts are usually tax free, but you need to check the law in your specific jurisdiction to confirm).

One benefit of both a whole life and a term policy is that the payout remains outside of the *probate* process; that is, it is not part of the legal proceedings associated with administering someone's estate upon death. The probate process can be lengthy, particularly if the estate is complicated, and the immediate payout on a life insurance policy can be especially helpful while the estate is tied up. A common example of this is when someone dies owing significant taxes. Because the estate is tied up in probate, the inheritors may not have access to sell the assets to pay taxes, or the assets may take a long time to sell. In this case, the payout can help fund any immediate taxes due.

You might have noticed that I have not done any financial calculations for pricing of life insurance, and that's deliberate. There is no way I could make any kind of meaningful example as there are too many factors that go into pricing. The pricing for life insurance depends on your age, health condition, amount of coverage, etc. But the key takeaway is that a term policy is much cheaper and can still provide you the coverage you need to protect your wealth.

How Much Life Insurance Do You Need?

This section will cover two different approaches to calculate how much life insurance you need. The first approach will quantify how much you need to replace your future earnings and the second approach will determine the present value of the future needs of your family.

Replacement of Your Future Earnings

This method captures the *present value* of your future before-tax earnings and adjusts for any expenses that will not exist once you are gone. Let's again use the example of the plumber from the "Quantifying the Cost" section of Chapter 9.

Assumptions:

Education Loan: $0 (as the training is mostly on the job there are no costs for school)

Work Years: 30 periods (it's currently the plumber's 28th birthday; assume the birthday falls on January 1, and the plumber will retire at the end of the year age 57)

Inflation Rate: 3% (the amount we discount future earnings by to get them in today's dollars; this will be compounded yearly)

Wage Inflation: 2%

Wage: $54,221 (starting salary of $44,480 for a plumber inflated by 2% for 10 years; refer back to the "Calculating the Future Value" section in Chapter 4 if you need a review)

Yearly Expense Decrease upon Death: $6,000 (assume you live with your significant other and upon your death household expenses for food, utilities, transportation, etc. will decrease by this amount)

We first need to calculate the pre-tax earnings adjusted for the decrease in annual expenses. Although taxes will likely not be charged on the lump sum payout from the insurance company, the reason we use pre-tax earnings is that we assume your beneficiary will invest the lump sum and use the returns to supplement their income back to the same level as when you were alive. As the beneficiary will owe taxes on the investment returns, we must calculate the lump sum on a before-tax basis.

As the calculation needs to be done separately for each year (i.e., 30 calculations), it is best tackled in Excel. However, I will use years 1 and 2 as an example to break down the calculations.

Year 1 (Age 28)
Inputs:

Earnings: $54,221 (the wage at age 28 from the assumptions above)

Yearly Expense Decrease: −$6,000 (negative because it is subtracted from earnings)

Discount Rate: $1.03^1 = (1 + \text{Inflation Rate})^{\text{Number of Periods}}$

Calculation:

Earnings after Expense Decrease: $54,221 − $6,000 = $48,221

Present Value of Pre-Tax Earnings: $48,221/1.03 = $46,816

Year 2 (Age 29)
Inputs:

Earnings: $55,305 (starting wage from previous year inflated by 2% [$54,221 * 1.02])

Yearly Expense Decrease: −$6,120 (previous year expense decrease inflated by 2% [$6,000 * 1.02]; this is negative because it is subtracted from earnings)

Discount Rate: $1.0609 = 1.03^2 = (1 + \text{Inflation Rate})^{\text{Number of Periods}}$

Calculation:

Earnings after Expense Decrease: $55,305 − $6,120 = $49,185

Present Value of Pre-Tax Earnings: $49,185/1.0609 = $46,362

Perform the same calculations for each subsequent period (i.e., 28 more times) and sum the present value of each year's earnings to get the amount of insurance you should purchase, which is $1,223,571.

These calculations are summarized in Exhibit 10.1 and can be found in detail on the "Replacement of Future Earnings" tab in the accompanying Excel file.

Exhibit 10.1 Replacement of Future Earnings Calculation Summary

Assumptions			Year 1	Year 2	Year 3		Year 28	Year 29	Year 30
Yearly Expense Decrease	($6,000)	**Age at Beginning of Year**	28	29	30		55	56	57
Work Years	30	**Full Year Earnings**	$54,221	$55,305	$56,411		$92,549	$94,400	$96,228
Inflation	3.00%	**Taxes**	($6,000)	($6,120)	($6,242)	....	($10,241)	($10,446)	($10,655)
Wage Inflation	2.00%	**Student Debt Repayment**	$0	$0	$0		$0	$0	$0
Starting Wage	$54,221	**Net Earnings**	$48,221	$49,185	$50,169		$82,308	$83,954	$85,633
Effective tax rate	15.00%	**Discount Rate Formula**	1.03^1	1.03^2	1.03^3		1.03^28	1.03^29	1.03^30
		Discount Rate	1.0300	1.0609	1.0927		2.2879	2.3566	2.4273
Present Value of Total Pre-Tax Earnings Adjusted for Expense Decrease	1,223,571	*Present Value of After Tax Earnings*	$46,816	$46,362	$45,912		$35,975	$35,625	$35,280

Needs Based

This method quantifies the future needs of your family and the goal is to make sure they are financially secure for the rest of their life. The calculation takes into account any outstanding debts you have, such as a mortgage and the costs of supporting your kids or significant other, and adjusts for any future earnings your spouse will have and any financial assets you have (stock portfolio, cash, etc.). Let's continue with the example for the family of plumbers and first look at any immediate cash needs using the following assumptions:

Assumptions:

Mortgage Debt: $300,000

Funeral Expenses: $10,000

Credit Card Debt: $6,000

The immediate cash needs total $316,000.

Next we look at any assets available to offset the immediate cash needs and use the following assumptions:

Assumptions:
    IRA: $50,000
    Cash in Savings Account: $15,000
    Work-Provided Life Insurance Policy: $5,000
    Financial assets available are $70,000, for a net immediate cash need of $246,000.

Next we look at the family's financial needs, which are the ongoing costs to support the child and spouse, using the following assumptions:

Assumptions:

    Spouse Living Expenses: $40,000 per year for 40 years (today is the spouse's 28th birthday, and he/she will need support for 40 years. The amount needed to support the spouse today is $40,000 and will increase by 4% every year)
    Child Expenses: $20,900 per year for 22 years (assume the child is just born and will need support until age 22; see Chapter 9 for additional details)
    Spouse After-Tax Income: $23,044 per year for 30 years (currently working half time and will work for 30 more years; see Chapter 9 for more details)

We need to calculate the present value for each of the above assumptions separately. Let's start with the spouse living expenses. The inputs are as follows:

Year 1 (Age 28)
Inputs:
    Living Expenses: $40,000
    Living Expense Inflation: 4% (living expenses include costs for food, utilities, clothes, property taxes, home and vehicle maintenance, health insurance, etc. As health insurance costs rise at a significantly higher pace than general inflation, and as these costs can make up a large proportion of living expenses, we assume living expenses increase at a rate slightly higher than general inflation)
    Inflation Rate: 3%

Calculation:
    Discount Rate: $1.03^1 = (1 + \text{Inflation Rate})^{\text{Number of Periods}}$
    Present Value of Living Expenses: $40,000/1.03 = $38,835

Year 2 (Age 29)

Inputs:

Living Expenses: $41,600 (year 1 inflated by 4% [$40,000 * 1.04])

Discount Rate: $1.0609 = 1.03^2 = (1 + \text{Inflation Rate})^{\text{Number of Periods}}$

Calculation:

Present Value of Living Expenses: $41,600/1.0609 = $39,212

We perform the same calculations as above for each subsequent period (i.e., 38 more times). The present value of future required living expenses is $1,887,143. A summary of the calculation is provided in Exhibit 10.2.

Exhibit 10.2 Present Value of Spouse Living Expenses Calculation Summary

Assumptions			Year 1	Year 2	Year 3	Year 28	Year 29	Year 30
Yearly Support Required	40	Age at Beginning of Year	28	29	30	65	66	67
Inflation Rate	3.00%	Living Expenses	$40,000	$41,600	$43,264	$170,724	$177,553	$184,655
Expense Inflation	4.00%	Discount Rate						
Living Expenses	$40,000	Formula	1.03^1	1.03^2	1.03^3	1.03^38	1.03^39	1.03^40
		Discount Rate	1.0300	1.0609	1.0927	3.0748	3.1670	3.2620
Present Value of Total Living Expenses	1,887,143	Present Value of After Tax Earnings	$38,835	$39,212	$39,593	$55,524	$56,063	$56,607

Next is the present value for the child expenses. As we have already calculated this in Chapter 9, I will not repeat the calculations here. The present value of expenses for the child is $495,002.

Lastly, we calculate the present value of the spouse's future earnings. Again, we have already calculated this in Chapter 9, so I will not repeat the calculations here. The present value of spousal future earnings is $584,722.

The next step is to combine the costs to support the child and spouse to get the net family financial needs, which is $1,797,422. This is spousal living expenses plus child cost minus spousal earnings ($1,887,143, + $495,002 − $584,722).

Finally, we combine the immediate cash need of $316,000, available assets of $70,000, and family financial needs of $1,797,422 for a total needs-based life insurance amount of $2,043,422 ($316,000 − $70,000 + $1,797,422).

As there are a lot of steps to this calculation, I have summarized it in Exhibit 10.3.

Exhibit 10.3 Needs Based Life Insurance Calculations Summary

Immediate Cash Needs

1	Outstanding Mortgage	($300,000)
	Funeral Expenses	($10,000)
	Credit Card Debt	($6,000)
	Total	($316,000)

Avaliable Assets

2	IRA	$50,000
	Cash in Savings Account	$15,000
	Work Sponsored Life Insurance Policy	$5,000
	Total	$70,000

Family Needs

3	Spouse Living Expenses ($40K per year until 68 years old)	($1,887,143)
	Child Expenses ($20,900 per year for 22 years, see Chapter 9 for details)	($495,002)
	Spouse After Tax Yearly Income (Current Half Time Salary, and will work for 30 more years)	$584,722
	Total	($1,797,422)

Summary

4	Immediate Cash Needs	($316,000)
	Avaliable Assets	$70,000
	Family Needs	($1,797,422)
	Total Needs Based Life Insurance	($2,043,422)

Taking a Policy for a Non-Working Spouse

This is important particularly if you have children and a non-working spouse who takes care of them. Some people may think, "If my spouse is not working, then why do I need to get insurance for him/her? He/she doesn't make any money." Trust me, no one is lining up around the block to take care of your kids 365 days a year for free. If something happens to your spouse, you will either have to pay someone to take care of them or take on the duties yourself. But working a full-time job and giving kids the attention they deserve, with no help, is not realistic. The exact amount you should insure your non-working spouse for is specific to each family. However, one way to estimate the economic value-add from a non-working spouse is to calculate the present value of hiring a full time live-in nanny until your kids are grown. In summary, insuring your non-working spouse is something you should strongly consider.

11

INVESTING FOR RETIREMENT

So, you are at a point in your life where you have some money saved and would like to invest. But you run into a problem: what the heck do you invest in? Bonds, stocks, real estate, gold, bitcoin – the list goes on.

Although I can't tell you exactly what to invest in or how much to invest, what I can do is help you think through the process in an organized and logical manner.

The steps are as follows:

Step 1: Define Your Goals

1. Clarify what you hope to achieve. Common answers include paying for your children's education, purchasing a vacation home, generating a certain amount of passive income, and donating to charity.

2. Quantify your goals. This acts as a sanity check of what you would like to do against what you can realistically achieve.

3. Prioritize your goals. Once you know what you want to achieve and how much it will cost, you can then prioritize the list.

Once you've defined your goals, you can create actionable steps to achieve them. The key is to develop a plan you can stick to, and to do that you have to understand what type of investor you are (very cautious and risk averse, risk seeking, or somewhere in between).

Defining yourself as an investor boils down to understanding how you will react emotionally when the market goes up or down. Emotions are not your friend when making a financial decision, as you need to think rationally. If you take your emotions into consideration when developing your plan, you can work to mitigate them; if you don't, it's unlikely you will stick to your plan and achieve your goals.

Step 2: Understand Your Investor Type

1. How do you perceive risk? Do you get excited when there is a lot of risk or do you freak out? If the thought of losing money makes you sick to the stomach, then you will not do well in high-risk/high-return investments. But if the thought of risk makes you excited, then high-risk/high-return investments could be just right for you.

2. What is your ability to bear risk? In other words, can you afford to lose money? If you have $50,000,000 to invest, and you put $50,000 in a high-risk/high-return investment, the likelihood of you not being able to meet your basic financial needs if the investment goes bust is extremely low. So your ability to bear risk is high. But if you have only $100,000 to invest and you lose $50,000, that's a huge blow to your net worth that you may not be able to recover from.

Step 3: Seek Help from an Investment Professional

Once you have completed steps 1 and 2, you can start honing in on some strategies. There is no way to provide an exhaustive list, as the combinations of goals and investor types are infinite, and I recommend you seek help from an investment professional to identify and manage a portfolio to meet your goals.

Putting the Retirement Investment Steps Together

Let's go through a hypothetical example so you can see how to think through the process.

Background

Jason is a computer programmer and Sarah is a school teacher. Both are 45 years old; they are married, have one child, and plan to retire at 60. Their combined income is $150,000/year (see Chapter 5, "Choosing the Right Career," for the median salaries of a computer programmer and a school teacher); they have $75,000 saved in cash, a primary residence, and two rental properties. Their daughter will start college in five years. Their primary residence and rental properties will be paid off on their 60th birthday, and at that point the rental properties will each generate $1,500 per month of income. Assume they have no other sources of income; that is, they have no *defined contribution plan*, defined benefits plan (i.e., company pension), inheritance, etc.

1. Define Goals
    *   What Do Jason and Sarah Hope to Achieve?
        o   Jason and Sarah's primary goal is to have enough passive income to maintain their current standard of living through retirement
        o   Their secondary goal is to fund their daughter's education

    *   Quantify Goals
        o   Their primary goal is to have $8,523 per month (see below for details) in pre-tax income and the time horizon is 15 years (i.e., their current age is 45 and they will retire at 60)
        o   Their secondary goal is to pay for their daughter's college and they expect a cost of $150,000 for tuition and lodging with a time horizon of five years (i.e., when their daughter will start college)

Exhibit 11.1 Retirement Income Requirement Summary

Combine Monthly Income	
Monthly Income (Pre Tax)	12,500
Current Income Tax Rate	20%
Monthly After Tax Income	**10,000**

Current Monthly Expenses	
Mortgage	-2,100
Property Taxes	-800
Utilities (Includes Water, Gas & Electric)	-500
Food	-1,500
Gym Membership	-100
Cell Phone & Internet	-150
Home Insurance	-100
Car Insurance	-100
Yard Maintenance	-100
Gas (for cars)	-300
Health Insurance	-500
Vacations	-500
Extracurricular Activities for child	-350
Misc (Car/Home Maintenance, Eating Out, etc.)	-400
Total Monthly Expenses	**-7,500**
Disposable Income	**2,500**

Assumptions	
Inflation Rate	3%
Retirement Income Tax Rate	15%
Year Until Retirement	15

Retirement Monthly Expenses (Today's Dollars)	
Mortgage	-0
Property Taxes	-800
Utilities (Includes Water, Gas & Electric)	-500
Food	-1,100
Gym Membership	-100
Cell Phone & Internet	-150
Home Insurance	-100
Car Insurance	-100
Yard Maintenance	-100
Gas (for cars)	-300
Health Insurance	-500
Vacations	-500
Extracurricular Activities for child	0
Misc (Car/Home Maintenance, Eating Out, etc.)	-400
Total Monthly Expenses	**-4,650**

Retirement Monthly Expenses (Future Dollars)	
Mortgage	0
Property Taxes	-1,246
Utilities (Includes Water, Gas & Electric)	-779
Food	-1,714
Gym Membership	-156
Cell Phone & Internet	-234
Home Insurance	-156
Car Insurance	-156
Yard Maintenance	-156
Gas (for cars)	-467
Health Insurance	-779
Vacations	-779
Extracurricular Activities for child	0
Misc (Car/Home Maintenance, Eating Out, etc.)	-623
Total Monthly Expenses	**-7,245**
Monthly Income Needed Before Tax	**8,523**

As Jason and Sarah's primary goal is to fund their retirement, let's focus on quantifying that objective first. To quantify a future income goal, we must calculate current expenses, amend for any changes in retirement, and adjust the amount for *inflation*. The calculations in Exhibit 11.1 show how I arrived at $8,523 per month for Jason and Sarah. These details can also be found in the "Retirement Income Estimator" tab in the accompanying Excel.

The left-hand box shows their monthly after-tax income ($10,000), monthly expenses (−$7,500), and disposable income ($2,500). The middle box shows their estimated retirement expenses, in today's dollars (−$4,650). Their retirement expenses are less than their current expenses as their house will be paid off (i.e., no mortgage payments) and their daughter will be supporting herself, so the food expense is reduced and the extracurricular activities go away. The box on the right shows their estimated retirement expenses 15 years from now (−$7,245). To calculate this figure, their retirement monthly expenses in today's dollars are inflated at 3% for 15 years (i.e., $4,650 * 1.03^{15}$). Lastly, their total monthly expenses must then be grossed up by their retirement tax rate of 15% as expenses are paid with after-tax dollars. So we divide $7,245 by (1 − 0.15), which is $8,523 per month. Also note the retirement tax rate is less (15% vs. 20%) than the tax rate when the couple is working. This is because their income will be lower, which will put them in a lower tax bracket.

Next, we must account for the two rental properties, which will be paid off at retirement. We first need to deduct the estimated rental income of $36,000 per year ($1,500 per month for two properties) from the yearly income needed of $102,276 ($8,523 * 12). This brings down the amount they need to generate from their retirement portfolio to $66,276 ($102,276 − $36,000).

2. Understand Investor Type
   a) Jason and Sarah are cautious investors. They have no investment experience and are willing to take medium to low risk. Also, they have only $75,000 to invest, so they cannot handle a large loss to their portfolio. In summary, Jason and Sarah decide their risk tolerance and ability to bear risk is medium to low.

Next let's look at some common investments to get an idea of the potential range of returns/degree of risk. Exhibit 11.2 ranks these investments from lowest to highest risk.

Exhibit 11.2 Investment Options Ranked from Lowest to Highest Risk

**Low Risk
Low Return**

Certificate of Deposit (CD): This is a time-based deposit account where a bank will give you a higher interest rate if you agree to lock up your money for some amount of time (the lockup period can range from 3 months to 10 years). Investopedia[15] has a great up-to-date summary of the best CD rates across the United States, and these rates range from less than 0.1% to approximately 1.5% depending on the bank and the time frame. CDs are offered by almost all banks, and as long as your bank is FDIC[16] insured these deposits are covered for up to $250,000.

U.S. Government Debt: These are bonds issued by the U.S. Treasury[17] and are generally considered risk free. The bonds come in a range of time horizons (1 week to 30 years) and also can be purchased with inflation protection. Depending on the time horizon, the returns for these bonds have typically ranged from less than 0.1% to around 3%.

**Medium Risk
Medium Return**

S&P 500 Index Fund: According to Investopedia,[18] the S&P 500 had an average return of approximately 10% per year from its inception through 2019. Keep in mind, however, that 10% is just a historical average and should not be taken as a guarantee of future returns. In any given year the actual return can be higher or lower than 10% (even negative), and over the short term there is likely to be significant volatility.

Market-Specific Funds: These are investment funds that track a specific subsection of the market (e.g., large cap, value, growth, dividend focused). As these portfolios get more concentrated, the risk, and also returns, potentially increase. Vanguard[19] has a broad selection of funds, and most importantly their management fees are extremely low. The average annual 10-year returns for Vanguard[19] funds range from about 1% to just under 20%; however, as I mentioned, historical returns should never be taken as a guarantee of future returns.

Individual Stocks or Corporate Bonds: Investing in the stocks or bonds of individual publicly traded companies requires a significant amount of research and due diligence, as there is considerably more volatility (i.e., potential for 100% losses to 100% and above returns) due to the concentrated risk.

**High Risk
High Return**

Derivatives: Derivatives are trading instruments that derive their value based on the performance of an underlying asset. Examples are options (e.g., puts and calls), swaps, swaptions, futures, and forward contracts. Derivatives can be extremely volatile (i.e., potential for greater than 100% loss to greater than 100% gain) and are typically only used by seasoned investors. The specifics of derivatives are beyond the scope of this book, but if you are interested in learning more, Investopedia[20] has a great derivatives 101 primer.

Portfolios are typically a blend of different investments, and as Jason and Sarah are cautious/low-risk investors, let's assume they choose a mix of medium- to low-risk options. We'll also assume a base case return, from their medium- to low-risk retirement portfolio, of 6% per year. We can now calculate the portfolio amount required, assuming a return of 6%, that will generate $66,276 per year by dividing $66,276 by 6% ($66,276/0.06), which is $1,104,600. See below for a summary of these assumptions, formulas, and calculations. See the "Retirement Portfolio Estimator" tab in the accompanying Excel file for detailed calculations.

Assumptions:

    Before-Tax Yearly Income Needed in Retirement: $102,276

    Income from Rental Properties: $36,000 per year (the two rental properties, which will be paid off when they retire, will generate this amount yearly)

    Investment Return: 6% (every year the investment portfolio will generate a return of 6%)

Formula:

    Portfolio Value = (Before-Tax Income − Income From Rental Properties)/Investment Return

Calculations:

    Portfolio Value = ($102,276 − $36,000)/0.06 = $66,276/0.06 = $1,104,600

Based on the above assumptions, Jason and Sarah need a portfolio of $1,104,600 to generate their desired retirement income. However, there is a chance that their returns in retirement will be higher or lower than 6% per year, and it's prudent to look at a range of scenarios (see Exhibit 11.3).

Exhibit 11.3

Portfolio Amount Needed to Generate Required Income	Assumed Rate of Return
$2,209,199	3%
$1,656,899	4%
$1,325,520	5%
$1,104,600	6%
$946,800	7%
$828,450	8%

If their portfolio returns only 3%, they will need approximately $2,200,000, but if the portfolio's returns are on the high end, at 8%, they will need only about $828,000.

Now that we have defined and quantified Sarah and Jason's goals and identified their ability and willingness to take risk, we can test how realistic each goal is and prioritize accordingly. First, let's test how likely it is Sarah and Jason can meet their retirement goal of $1,104,600. Again, we'll assume a 6% return on any money they invest and use the FV (future value) calculation in Excel to test whether they can meet their goal by saving their current disposable income. See the "Future Value of Investment" tab in the accompanying Excel file for detailed calculations. The assumptions and inputs are as follows:

Assumptions:

Rate: 6% (expected return from their investments)

Periods: 15 (15 years until they plan to retire)

Disposable Income: $30,000 per year ($2,500 per month * 12)

Initial Investment: $75,000 (the amount Sarah and Jason currently have saved and will invest immediately; assume this is invested on January 1)

Inputs:

The FV function in Excel takes the following arguments:

Rate (Interest Rate): 0.06 (how much the investments are expected to grow by each year)

Nper (Number of Periods): 15 (the number of yearly investments they will make)

PMT (Payment): −$30,000 (disposable income they will invest each year)

PV (Present Value): −$75,000 (the initial investment amount; this is negative because they must invest this amount)

Type: 0 (this means they invest the $30,000 at the end of each year)

At the end of 15 years, the investments will grow to $878,021. This is well below their goal of $1,104,600. Based on the above assumptions, we can use the PMT (payment) formula in Excel to see how much per year they need to invest to achieve a future value of $1,104,600. The inputs used in this Excel function are as follows:

Inputs:

Rate (Interest Rate): 0.06 (how much the investments are expected to grow by each year)

Nper (Number of Periods): 15 (the number of yearly investments they will make)

PV (Present Value): $75,000 (the amount initially invested)

FV (Future Value): $1,104,600 (the amount they want to have at retirement)

Type: 0 (this means they invest at the beginning of each year)

They need to invest $55,179 per year to reach the goal of $1,104,600.

At this point, Jason and Sarah need to reassess their goal as it is not realistic given the amount they can save and their ability and willingness to bear risk. Based on the sensitivity analysis above, only in the best-case scenario, with a return of 8%, can they achieve their primary retirement goal with investing only $30,000 per year. At this point the couple has several options:

- Delay retirement: This will allow them to save more and allow longer for their investments to grow

- Increase yearly savings: Decrease monthly expenses and increase disposable income; they could also take on second jobs to generate additional investment income
- Lower retirement income needs: They can either lower their retirement standard of living or retire to a cheaper location where they can maintain the same standard of living (i.e., retire abroad)

One or any combination of the above options can be used to meet their retirement goals. If Jason and Sarah still insist on paying for their daughter's college, they also have the options of sending their daughter to a cheaper college or delaying when their daughter starts college to give their portfolio more time to grow.

Now that Jason and Sarah have prioritized their goals and identified their risk tolerance and ability to bear risk, an investment advisor will be able to help them hone in on the specific portfolio that will best meet their needs. There are many types of financial advisors and levels of financial services to accommodate all investors. Depending on your level of wealth, the advisor services you can expect are broadly as follows (ordered from smallest to largest amount of investable assets):

1. Algorithm-based advisory (also known as Robo Advisors): This is for the lowest level of assets ($0 to $25,000) and provides algorithm-based financial services. You will likely complete an online survey specifying your investable assets, goals, risk tolerance, etc. and then, based on your responses, a computer algorithm will recommend investments for you. This helps companies reduce cost and provide services that would otherwise be too costly for smaller accounts.

2. Algorithm-based advisory with some degree of professional management. Level of assets: $25,000 to $200,000. The exact level of professional management will differ depending on your investable amount and the particular company you are using.

3. Professionally managed custom portfolios. Level of assets: $200,000 to $1,000,000. At this level, there will be a dedicated wealth manager looking after your portfolio.

4. Professionally managed custom portfolios. Level of assets: $1,000,000+. At this level, the client to wealth manager ratio decreases, and as your wealth increases, you get increasingly personalized services such as tax, legal, and estate planning.

The exact amounts required for investment and level of service will differ based on the advisor you use. Most financial services companies, such as E-Trade,[21] Vanguard,[22] TD Ameritrade,[23] Fidelity,[24] and a range of boutique firms, offer advisory services, and you can find more detail regarding offerings on their websites.

As an aside, many people hesitate to reveal their financial situation to others as it can be scary or even embarrassing. However, when you meet with a financial advisor, I encourage you not to hold anything back. It's important to remember that advisors are there to help, not judge, and the more clearly they understand your situation the better they can assist you.

The main takeaway from this chapter is that by going through the above steps, you can better determine what to realistically expect from your financial situation. In addition, if you can articulate your goals and risk preferences, and if the goals are realistic, you will not only manage your own expectations, but put your financial advisor in the best position to help you.

FINAL THOUGHTS

Ideally, if we just worked hard and paid our bills on time, we could all be financially secure. But the reality is that a certain degree of financial literacy and the ability to make informed financial decisions is a requirement in today's society. Far too many people are not equipped with the tools to navigate life's important financial decisions, and this lack of a financial toolset puts many people at risk of a lifetime of hard work with little to show for it.

Congratulations on completing the book. Financial knowledge is a journey, and by reading this book, you've taken an important step on that journey. The concepts I've covered are essential for everyday life, and developing an understanding of these ideas will set you on a path to future success. As I continue my own pursuit of financial knowledge, I will continue to share insights I gain through future materials. I wish you the best and thank you for letting me be a part of your financial journey.

Downloadable Excel file password: 2$&6gMyP0*86

RECOMMENDED READING & ADDITIONAL RESOURCES

Recommended Reading

- *The Millionaire Next Door,* Thomas J. Stanley & William D. Danko
- *Rich Dad Poor Dad,* Robert T. Kiyosaki
- *The Strategic Dividend Investor,* Daniel Peris
- *How to Invest in Real Estate: The Ultimate Beginner's Guide to Getting Started,* Brandon Turner & Joshua Dorkin

Additional Resources

- MichaelTortorichFinance.com
- MichaelTortorichFinance YouTube (www.youtube.com/channel/UCVsE6t24aI_c6s-pSgDKqhw)
- Investopedia.com
- Seekingalpha.com

GLOSSARY

Accrued Interest: Interest on a loan that has been incurred and not yet paid.

Actively Managed Fund: An investment fund where management uses a proprietary strategy to earn a higher return. These funds charge higher management fees than index funds as you are paying for the managers' skill and the potential for higher returns.

Adjustable-Rate Mortgage: A combination of a fixed-rate and a variable-rate loan. There are many different options, such as 3-, 5-, and 7-year fixed. After the initial fixed-rate period, during which the rate is typically lower than for a standard fixed-rate amortizing loan, the rate resets to a predetermined benchmark plus a markup and continues to reset periodically throughout the life of the loan.

Amortizing Loan: A loan where fixed payments are made over a predefined period until the loan is paid off.

Annual Percentage Rate (APR): Yearly interest rate.

Annual Percentage Yield (APY): Effective interest rate based on the frequency at which the Annual Percentage Rate (APR) is calculated.

Assets Under Management: The value of an investment that a fund manages on behalf of its investors.

Average Daily Balance Method: A method of charging interest on credit cards that calculates interest based on the weighted average balance outstanding for the billing cycle.

Compound Interest: Interest charged on interest.
Formula:
Principal $* \{(1 + \text{Interest Rate})^{\text{Number of Periods}}\}$

Credit Report: A report that contains your payment history, debt outstanding, length of credit history, credit mix, and any new credit.

Credit Score: A number issued by various rating agencies (see usa.gov/credit-reports for more details) that indicates your creditworthiness (i.e., how likely you are to pay back your loans and pay them back on time). The score is calculated based on many factors, including how much debt you have and your payment history (i.e., do you frequently pay your bills on time or do you have a history of late or delinquent payments?). A higher score indicates you are more likely to pay back your debt and usually results in a lower interest rate (because the risk premium assessed is lower).

Daily Balance Method: A method of charging interest on credit cards that calculates interest daily based on the balance outstanding each day in the billing cycle.

Daily Periodic Rate: Annual Percentage Rate (APR) divided by 360 or 365 (the exact number of days used depends on your specific loan terms).

Defined Contribution Plan: An employer-offered, usually tax-deferred, retirement plan where an employee contributes a percentage of their salary into a retirement account. Typically, the account is tax advantaged, a portion of the employee contribution is matched by the employer, and the funds are restricted for some period of time.

Discount Rate: Rate used to discount future cash flows back to their current value.

Escrow Account: An account managed by a third party that holds funds for real estate property taxes and insurance.

401(k): An employer-offered, tax-deferred retirement plan where an employee contributes a percentage of their salary into a retirement account. A portion of the employee contribution is usually matched by the employer, and the funds are restricted (i.e., you cannot withdraw without penalty) until age 59½. Contributions are capped depending on the employee's age and tax year (the amount is usually adjusted upward for inflation each year). As of 2020, for employees under 50 years old the yearly contribution limit was $19,500.

Front-End Ratio: Shows what percentage of your income is going to pay your mortgage. Calculated as (Promissory Note Repayment + Property Tax + Insurance)/Gross Income.

Index: A theoretical portfolio of investments that tracks the performance of some segment of the financial market. You cannot invest directly in an index and in most cases have to invest in an index fund that will purchase the investments to replicate a particular Index.

Index Fund: A fund constructed to track a certain index by purchasing the specified investments. You cannot invest directly in an index, and typically it is unrealistic for an individual to purchase and maintain all the investments represented in a particular index due to the cost and required technical expertise. Index funds allow individual investors to pool their money and outsource the maintenance to a financial professional.

Inflation: Decrease in purchasing power over time. As prices rise, $1.00 tomorrow cannot buy the same amount of goods or services as $1.00 today.

Interest: Additional amount you have to pay back when you borrow money. Interest includes two components: risk and inflation.

Interest-Only Loan: A type of loan where the borrower pays only interest on the principal. The monthly payments are less than for an amortizing loan as no principal portion is included in the monthly payments. At the end of the term the full principal amount must be repaid.

Interest Rate: Amount owed in addition to principal, stated as a percentage.

Investment Fund: An investment vehicle where investors pool their money and outsource the supervision to an experienced management team.

Liquid The ease with which an investment can be converted into cash.

Minimum Payment: Minimum amount you have to pay on the outstanding balance of your credit card each month. In most cases, if you pay only the minimum balance, you will never pay off your credit card.

Mortgage: A document that allows the lender to repossess and sell your house if you don't repay your loan.

Opportunity Cost: The value of what you give up (the next-best alternative) by choosing a specific option.

Period: Interval at which interest is charged (e.g., daily, weekly, monthly, yearly).

Periodic Interest Rate: Annual interest rate divided by the number of periods in one year.

Present Value: Current value of future money. Because of inflation, the same amount of money will have less buying power in the future than today. Present value adjusts future money to today's value.

Prime Rate: Interest rate banks charge to their most creditworthy customers.

Principal: Amount that you originally borrowed.

Probate: The legal process of administering someone's estate after death.

Promissory Note: The actual contract you sign to borrow money for a house.

Refinancing: Taking a loan out at a lower interest rate to pay off an existing loan with a higher interest rate.

Revolving Account: The most common types of revolving accounts are credit cards and home equity lines of credit. Unlike a loan that requires fixed payments over a predetermined payback period, these accounts have a maximum credit limit with no maturity date and flexible repayment terms.

Risk: Uncertainty. In financial terms, risk is the uncertainty around getting paid back in full the money you are owed.

Risk Premium: Additional amount charged as part of interest for the risk of not getting paid back

Simple Interest: Non-compounding interest.

Tax Deferred: Contributions are not taxed until the money is withdrawn.

Tax Drag: Taxes paid over the life of an investment.

NOTES

Chapter 3: Credit Cards

[1] Consumer Financial Protection Bureau (https://www.consumerfinance.gov/consumer-tools/credit-reports-and-scores/); myFICO https://www.myfico.com/credit-education/credit-scores

Chapter 5: Choosing the Right Career

[2] Williams, O.E., Lacasa, L., & Latora, V. "Quantifying and predicting success in show business." *Nat Commun* 10, 2256 (2019). https://doi.org/10.1038/s41467-019-10213-0

[3] https://www.usnews.com/education/best-colleges/paying-for-college/articles/paying-for-college-infographic

[4] https://www.bls.gov/ooh/

[5] https://studentaid.gov/manage-loans/repayment/plans/standard

Chapter 6: Paying Off Student Loans

[6] https://www.daveramsey.com/blog/how-the-debt-snowball-method-works

Chapter 7: Defined Contribution Plans

[7] https://www.irs.gov/retirement-plans/plan-sponsor/types-of-retirement-plans

[8] https://www.irs.gov/retirement-plans/plan-participant-employee/retirement-topics-401(k)-and-profit-sharing- plan-contribution-limits

[9] https://money.cnn.com/retirement/guide/

[10] https://www.investopedia.com/ask/answers/042214/how-can-i-fund-roth-ira-if-my-income-too-high-make-direct-contributions.asp

Chapter 8: Purchasing a House

[11] https://www.poconnor.com/

[12] https://www.investopedia.com/mortgage/mortgage-guide/mortgage-insurance/

[13] https://www.investopedia.com/articles/pf/05/030905.asp

[14] https://www.investopedia.com/mortgage-preapproval-4776405

Chapter 11: Investing for Retirement

[15] https://www.investopedia.com/best-cd-rates-4770214

[16] https://www.fdic.gov/deposit/covered/#:~:text=FDIC%20insurance%20covers%20all%20types,a%20bank%2C%20such%20as%20a

[17] https://www.treasurydirect.gov/indiv/products/products.htm

[18] https://www.investopedia.com/ask/answers/042415/what-average-annual-return-sp-500.asp

[19] https://investor.vanguard.com/etf/list#/etf/asset-class/month-end-returns

[20] https://www.investopedia.com/articles/optioninvestor/10/derivatives-101.asp

[21] https://us.etrade.com/planning/personalized-investments

[22] https://investor.vanguard.com/advice/financial-advisor/

[23] https://www.tdameritrade.com/investment-products/managed-portfolios.page

[24] https://www.fidelity.com/managed-accounts/overview

ABOUT THE AUTHOR

Michael Tortorich has a bachelor's degree and an MBA from the University of Texas at Austin McCombs School of Business. He has 10-plus years of corporate finance experience and most importantly is a passionate believer in promoting financial literacy. The content in this book was originally designed as a financial education course for his two children, but after completion he decided to turn the material into a book that anyone could benefit from.

Made in the USA
Las Vegas, NV
29 July 2021

27244939R00057